S0-CNB-891

Stewardship of Creation

William C. Crouser

STEWARDSHIP OF CREATION is the second in a series of program resources for outdoor ministry that are being produced through the work of the Committee on Outdoor Ministries of the National Council of the Churches of Christ in the U.S.A. These resources include *Community,* ready for 1986 camps, and *Lifestyles of Faithfulness,* introduced last year for church camps and conferences in 1984 and 1987.

STEWARDSHIP OF CREATION is composed of four resource books for camp counselors and program leaders.

- **Basic Resource Guide,** which introduces the theme and presents activities, projects, and planning helps on the theme. This guide is designed to be used in camps that include all ages (intergenerational camps). Its resources can be easily adapted for use in camps for specific age groups.
- **Guide for Older Children** (ages 8–11)
- **Guide for Younger Youth** (ages 12–14)
- **Guide for Older Youth** (ages 15–18)

These three supplemental guides contain resources for camps and conferences using the "Stewardship of Creation" theme that are especially appropriate for these three age groups. The guides are designed to be used in conjunction with the *Basic Resource Guide* both in camps for older children, younger youth, and older youth and in intergenerational camps during those times when these age groups will need to meet apart from the other age levels. Each guide discusses the special needs of the age group and presents planning suggestions as well as program activities.

In addition to these program resources, which are part of the *Sow Seeds, Trust the Promise* materials produced by the NCCC, two other books in the *Sow Seeds, Trust the Promise* collection will provide helpful resources for camp leaders and administrators:

- *Leadership Development Notebook* provides leader-training units on theology, faith development, understanding of self and community, leader skills, and planning/resourcing.
- *Administrative Manual* for camp boards, committees, and administrators provides helps for policymakers of church camps and conference centers in all the major facets of their responsibilities.

These two resources are available from your denominational publishing house or religious bookstore.

ISBN 0-664-24489-0   Printed in the United States of America

Contents

Cover by Gene Harris

William C. Crouser is director of Lutheran Outdoor Ministries
of Northern California. He is also director of a camp and
conference center near Santa Cruz, California.

1.
Introduction

THE THEME: OUR STEWARDSHIP
OF GOD'S CREATION

In many parts of the North American continent increasing population and resource-consuming life-styles are creating pressures to use highly productive agricultural lands for other purposes. As population grows, more land is needed for houses, highways, businesses, recreation, and industrial areas.

Most people agree that it is both necessary and legitimate to use land for these purposes in addition to providing adequate land for agriculture. But the trend toward converting prime, or highly productive, farmland to nonagricultural uses is alarming. Prime farmland is level, well drained, with adequate supplies of water and sunshine—qualities that make it highly desirable for nonagricultural purposes as well. It has been estimated that currently in the United States four square miles of prime farmland are being shifted to uses other than agriculture every day. In California, for example, urban dovolopmcnt io rcducing the agricultural land base by an estimated 20,000 acres annually. And farmland in Minnesota has been converted to nonfarm use at the rate of 273 acres a day! How does that compare to the size of your camp?

Even in Canada, where 43 percent of the country is still timbered, the southern agricultural area has lost two thirds of its forests since colonization began. Of the original volume of 3,648 billion cubic feet of timber, only 1,094 billion remained as early as 1912. Many agricultural projects have been abandoned because of the subsequent soil erosion.

Surprisingly enough, much of the land taken out of agricultural production has not been paved over with the classic suburban sprawl. About 27 percent has been covered by factories, highways, parking lots, expensive lawns, and other signs of modern civilization. But the balance of the land has been taken out of farm production for "parcelization": large farms are broken up into smaller "ranchette" parcels and sold to people who want a spread of land but are not actually going to farm it.

Another factor in the loss of prime agricultural land is erosion. About 10 percent of the earth's land surface is suitable for farming. Within the past century, one quarter of the soil on that land has been eroded—mainly as a result of overgrazing and overfarming. In the United States, erosion of topsoil is so serious that the soil lost each year would cover the state of Iowa with a layer of dirt one inch thick!

Years ago a Blackfoot chieftain said, "Our land is more valuable than your money. It will last forever. It will not perish by the flames of fire. As long as the sun shines and the water flows, this land will be here to give life to men and animals. . . . You can count your money and burn it within the nod of a buffalo's head, but only the Great Spirit can count the grains of sand and the blades of grass of these plains. As a present to you, we will give you anything we have that you can take with you, but the land, never."

What would the chieftain say today? The thin layer of topsoil that supports our life is being diminished far more rapidly than it is being replenished. Water is being withdrawn from the ground at a rate of 82 billion gallons each day while only 61 billion gallons soak into the ground from the sky during the same period. And the air is being invaded with poisonous wastes, which return to us as smog, acid rain, and other noxious pollutants.

Malnutrition also affects us. Hunger (undernutrition) results when people consume fewer calories and less protein than their bodies need to live active, healthy lives. Undernutrition also increases susceptibility to disease. For instance, in the next sixty seconds 234 babies will be born in the world—136 in Asia, 41 in Africa, 23 in Latin America, and 34 in the rest of the world. Of those 234 babies, 23 will die before their first birthday—14 of the 136 in Asia, 6 of the 41 in Africa, 2 of the 23 in Latin America, and perhaps 1 of the other 34. Fifty to 75 percent of those deaths can be attributed to a combination of malnutrition and infectious diseases. Many who do survive beyond the age of fifteen will be stunted in physical growth and suffer brain damage that will incapacitate them for life. Malnutrition results from a lack of essential vitamins and minerals, usually from not eating enough of the right kinds of food. For example, 100,000 children go blind each year because of a lack of vitamin A in their diet. As strange as it may sound, malnutrition in the United States is often the result of eating too much so-called junk food.

To top it all off, we are rapidly using up many of our conventional energy sources, including firewood in many parts of the world, and we are threatening to blow one another apart with all sorts of nuclear weapons!

In *Rom. 8:18-23,* the apostle Paul wrote of creation with words like "suffer," "pain," "longing," "slavery to decay," and "groaning." This is a rather dismal set of words for something that we usually view as being beautiful. Yet when we think of land erosion, chemical contamination, worldwide hunger, and the possibilities of nuclear destruction, we are apt to say that Paul understated the situation.

On the other hand, creation was not always viewed so negatively. In *Gen., ch. 1,* we are told that "in the beginning, when God created the universe . . ." with "all kinds of plants, those that bear grain and those that bear fruit . . ." and "all kinds of animal life: domestic and wild, large and small . . ." and finally ". . . God created human beings, . . . male and female . . . ," then "God looked at everything he had made, and he was very pleased." Another translation of Genesis says that Almighty God saw, in looking at creation, "that it was very good"! (King James Version.)

What has happened to change this picture of beauty and perfection to one of dust and despair? Quite simply, sin came into the world because of the disobedience of humankind. And God said, "Because of what you have done, the ground will be under a curse. . . . It will produce weeds and thorns, and you will have to eat wild plants." *(Gen. 3:17-18.)* People would not get their living free anymore, from God's beautiful Garden of Eden. From that point onward they would sweat and toil to gain a living from the soil.

Very clearly, sin is the breaking of the relationship with God, one's self, one's neighbor, and the whole of creation, and we are all guilty of transgressing God's will in thought, word, and deed. This guilt can be removed only by the life, death, and resurrection of Jesus Christ, and we must not allow our understanding and acceptance of this Biblical truth to be diluted in any respect. Particularly in our stewardship of creation, we must be in a right relationship with God if we are not to plunder the earth, but to care for it properly.

God knew that humanity would sin. Still, we were given a tremendous stewardship responsibility: dominion *(Gen. 1:28,* RSV) over the earth and every living thing in it. Dominion is a strong word; it brings to mind a kindly ruler, caring for each and every thing in the kingdom.

As part of God's people, we will have a deep concern about how we use the earth over which we have been given dominion, attempting to exercise wisdom and compassion in our relationships with the whole world and all its inhabitants. "Human beings are responsible for a complex web of biological, cultural, and political systems. In Jesus' teaching, 'The steward was at any moment accountable, not primarily for the profits he earned for his master, but for the faithfulness of his dealings with the servants as well as with the goods *(Luke 12:41 ff.).*'"[1] God's stewards will not devastate the earth, but will be inspired by the vision of God's "shalom," the Biblical vision of peace, harmony, and universal well-being on earth. That vision is described in the creation accounts *(Gen. 1:1 to 2:3; 2:4-25)* and expanded in such passages as *Ps. 85:8-13; Ps. 104; Isa. 11:1-9; 65:17-25;* and *Col. 1:9-23.* "Dominion" means that we will preserve and protect all that is precious in God's sight so that future generations also can enjoy all of God's gifts. Faithful stewards, in other words, will be good managers.

This is quite a stewardship ideal to live up to! And, of course, most of us recognize that we have failed. In our Judeo-Christian tradition (and out in the larger world too) humanity has ganged up on nature. Here is an example: In the fifth chapter of I Kings we read that King Solomon sent ten thousand men each month to Lebanon to cut down and hew cedar and cypress trees into lumber for the Temple. Later he continued the harvesting and used the lumber in commerce with other countries. Today only a few trees remain in that area of the world.

Even before the Bible was written, erosion from human activities was known in ancient China. Almost universally men and women have disturbed the ecological equilibrium out of ignorance, chiefly because they were more concerned with immediate advantage than with long-range goals. Grazing by domesticated animals is one example. According to René Dubos, "The goat has helped countless human beings to survive by its ability to derive nourishment from poor lands, but it has probably contributed even more than modern bulldozers to the destruction of the land and the creation of deserts."[2]

Modern humanity has quite readily accepted freedom from religious bondage to nature—certainly we do not worship nature anymore—but too often in our freedom we have become arrogant and have forgotten how much a part of nature we really are.

The question we will try to answer in this book is, What can we do to return nature to the glory of creation, to restore the brokenness, so that once again

---

[1] From *Energy Ethics: A Christian Response,* ed. by Dieter Hessel. Friendship Press, 1979. The inner quotation is from a study paper, "Economic Justice Within Environmental Limits," by Charles West, published in *Church and Society,* September–October 1976.

[2] From "The Genius of the Place," by René J. Dubos, printed in condensed form in *American Forests,* September 1970.

Almighty God can take joy in it and see that it is good?

I know what you are probably thinking: How can I, one person, even surrounded by other interested people in a camp, hope to improve the lot of creation, or make a dent in the environmental crisis?

First, accept the responsibility of stewardship, and try. Yes, you may fail at times. We all do. But try again. Start small, within your own sphere of influence—your cabin, your camp—and expand later as you have opportunity. Keep close to the Lord. Your relationship to heaven will invariably affect your relationship with the earth.

Remember your responsibility! Do not be just a steward; be a *just* steward of God's creation.

THE VALUES OF INTERGENERATIONAL CAMPING

This entire resource book was written with the idea that in many camps it will be used in an intergenerational setting. I am enthusiastic about intergenerational programming because I have experienced it at work in our camp. I believe church camps now have a unique opportunity to help persons of all ages and backgrounds as they worship together in the family of God, live together in forgiving love, and work and play together for a common goal.

In your camp a caring and supportive community can develop as staff and campers are affirmed and then challenged to learn from one another. Younger children can often stimulate enthusiastic participation by older members of the group by their own openness and curious questions. Senior members of the new community will be happy to pass on knowledge that they have gathered from years of experience. Teenagers, when allowed the freedom to join in the group on their own terms, will find this a safe setting in which to relax and enjoy simple games and activities with much younger children or to stretch themselves against the values and knowledge of older participants.

Actually, intergenerational camp programming is an old idea with a fairly new twist. All over the world intergenerational experiences take place quite naturally every day. This is particularly true among primitive societies and in most of the developing nations where clan, tribal, and village members depend on one another to a very high degree for their well-being and, in many cases, for their very lives.

In the culture in which Jesus lived there was already an effort to separate the age groups. You will remember that even Jesus' disciples scolded the people who brought their children to be with the Lord. But when Jesus noticed this he was angry, and he said to his disciples, "Let the children come to me, and do not stop them, because the Kingdom of God belongs to such as these" (*Mark 10:14*).

Before the United States and Canada developed the mobile societies in which we find ourselves today, with a high degree of departmentalization even in the church, it was not unusual for three or four generations to live and work together on the same land or at least in the same community. And so intergenerational activities were a natural part of everyday life. It was not unusual for children, parents, aunts and uncles, cousins and grandparents to form natural bonds of love and concern for one another.

Within this century, with more rapid transportation available, and with individuals encouraged to spread out across the country to find new vocational opportunities in a technological society, many of the positive contributions of the natural extended family have been lost for a great many of our people.

I believe that our camps are "at the right place at the right time" to effectively meet the needs of people of all ages through intergenerational camping. As we develop an extended family of faith, we can provide role models for campers of all ages, we can show concern and provide support in times of crisis, we can pass on to future generations the knowledge and skills we have acquired, and we can lovingly share our Christian faith.

It seems to me that intergenerational programming is important if we are going to be faithful to the teachings of the Bible. We should be in one community, for "Christ is like a single body, which has many parts; it is still one body, even though it is made up of different parts. In the same way, all of us, whether Jews or Gentiles, whether slaves or free, have been baptized into the one body by the same Spirit, and we have all been given the one Spirit to drink" (*I Cor. 12:12-13*).

Within the one body the older members clearly have the responsibility to keep the faith and to share it with the younger members. Very clearly, the Bible tells us that the faith is to be passed on, and if we fail to do this, it may be lost forever. "Love the Lord your God with all your heart, with all your soul, and with all your strength. Never forget these commands that I am giving you today. Teach them to your children. Repeat them when you are at home and when you are away, when you are resting and when you are working." (*Deut. 6:5-7.*)

By the same token, children have something to share with their elders. Jesus said, "I assure you that whoever does not receive the Kingdom of God like a child will never enter it." (*Mark 10:15.*) And Isaiah plainly foretold the shalom time when he stressed, "He will rule his people with justice and integrity. Wolves and sheep will live together in peace, and leopards will lie down with young goats. Calves and lion cubs will feed together, and little children will take care of them" (*Isa. 11:5-7*). How true this appears today when things are changing so rapidly in the world that, for the most part, only the young can keep up. And though it is the older generations who must pass on the old word to the young, the younger generations must help the older generation understand the developing word. Both are God's word, and they are one!

CONCERNS AND CHARACTERISTICS OF THE GENERATIONS

In making your program plans, there are some definite age-group concerns about which you should be aware. I am going to list some age-group characteristics and needs along with important events and relationships as I have found them. As you review the list, you can add more from your personal and collective experience. (You see, I hope you are already working on this program as a group of leaders.) The list is on the next two facing pages.

Most program planners separate the participants into various age groupings and call them "generations." You may have defined the term differently, but it seems to me that in this time of rapid change even three or four years' difference in age can mean a different "generation" in outlook and experience, particularly for school-age children, youth, and young adults. I must confess, too, that as I have grown older it appears to me that middle age starts later and lasts longer.

For the purpose of what follows in this book, when I use the term *generation* I mean five broad age groups in the human life span:

Generation	Important Life Events	Important Relationships
Children Younger children (Birth to age 5 or 6)	Birth, baptism Feeding, teething, weaning First step, first word Entering church, nursery school	Parenting person, family Day care and nursery leaders Grandparents, relatives Neighborhood, family friends Kindergarten teacher
Elementary children (Grades 1 to 6)	Entering school Learning to read Learning to ride a bike Joining clubs, Scouts Onset of puberty	School teachers and friends Church leaders and friends Club and activity leaders, peers Media personalities, sports figures Same-sex close friends
Youth Early adolescents (Grades 7 to 8/9)	Entering a new school Confirmation First dates Scholastic success/failure Sexual experiences	Peer cliques, gangs Teammates Significant adult leaders Opposite-sex friends Church fellowship groups
Senior highs (Grades 9/10 to 12)	Entering high school First job Driver's license Getting a car High school commencement	Romantic relationships Community leaders, public figures Adult friends
Young adults (After high school to 30 or 35)	Entering vocational training or college First full-time employment Graduation from training or college Leaving home Marriage or cohabitation First child born Relating anew to church and community Establishing a career Moving to a different area Children entering school Last child born	Teachers Career models Peers of the same life-style Sexual relationships Boss and work associates Spouse In-laws Children
Middle adults (30/35 to 60/65)	Job promotions Church and community leadership Marriage crisis; divorce First child leaves home First child marries Menopause 25th anniversary First grandchild Career plateau Last child leaves home New career Death of parents Retirement	Neighbors, friends Children's friends and their parents Work associates Spouse One's children as youth Community agencies Public figures One's children as young adults More in-laws Grandchildren
Older adults (Over 60/65)	New leisure activities 50th anniversary Move to retirement community Death of spouse Remarriage Serious illness Move to nursing home or relatives' Death	Spouse One's children as adults Church and club friends New group of older friends Great-grandchildren

Needs and Concerns	Gifts to Share
Food, sleep, protection, warmth, cleanliness Care, attention, response, holding, exercise Toilet training, acceptance of body Free exploration within limits Play with peers, expression of feeling Secure base of family support Various experiences in rich environment	Helplessness Charm Rapid growth Response to love Curiosity Openness in thoughts, feelings
Development of learning skills Exercise and coordination of large muscles Satisfying, self-directed work Dealing with success and failure Skill in peer group relations Experiences of care, service to others Challenge of ideas and self-investment	Industry Rapid learning Vitality Imagination Expanding interests
Understanding and acceptance of pubescent changes Enriching peer relationships with both sexes Exposure to social issues Experiences of success Self-esteem, self-understanding	Enthusiasm, passion Questioning attitude Loyalty to friends Idealism Physical strength, coordination
Supportive adults, "adult guarantors" Increasing freedom and responsibility Opportunities to test roles, values, self-image Clarified values, sharper commitments	Commitment to causes Growing competence
Responsibility for one's affairs Sense of vocational direction Close personal relationship with a few others Maturing relationship with one's parents Growing abilities in daily work; promotions Maturing sense of one's role in history/society Fidelity to loved ones Capacity to care for children	Willingness to risk Expanding knowledge Creativity Intimacy
Financial security for one's family Marital adjustments Heavy demands of child rearing Creative, productive work in job and community Self-esteem in the face of disappointments, doubt Care and support for children in their new freedom Care of aged parents Exploration of new work and service options	Dependability, steadiness Concern for the future Financial resources
Major adjustment to retirement Sufficient financial support Creative and useful investment of time Acceptance by persons and institutions Review and affirmation of one's life Human sharing in grief, joy, confusion Close relationships dwindling through death Increasing health care Limited mobility	More time Wisdom, objectivity Person-centeredness Triumph over suffering Acceptance of death Hope

From *Learning Together*, by George E. Koehler, Discipleship Resources, the United Methodist Church, P.O. Box 840, Nashville, Tenn. 37202.

- Children (birth through about the sixth grade)
- Youth (roughly seventh through twelfth grades)
- Young Adults (from high school graduation till about age thirty or thirty-five)
- Middle Age (from thirty or thirty-five to sixty-five or retirement)
- Older Adults (beyond sixty-five, or retirement if this comes later)

GROUPING

I have already stressed the role of various generations in the development of one another's faith. In a relational camp program made up of all ages, we should all become aware of God's love for us and then respond in faith and love. The camp setting can help us discover God's good news for Earth, start to understand others' concerns for the whole creation, and decide to assume some responsibility for the world of tomorrow. Briefly stated, campers can come to know the gospel, the world situation, and the relationship between the two!

The intergenerational setting will provide the nourishment and affirmation needed by each of us. You cannot plan this, but you can plan for it. It happens as we live life together—as we pray, eat, play, work, hike, sing, challenge, and serve with one another.

There are several different ways to plan for your intergenerational program, particularly in dividing up the whole camp population into more manageable units. I have discovered that the most effective plan calls for two or more different types of groupings every day. Here are some sample types of groupings. You can discover more as you consider your site, the available facilities, the number and backgrounds of participants, and so forth.

Learning Community Groups. In this style of oganization, campers work together at a single task—for example, some get-acquainted activity or a worship experience. Smaller groups of twenty-five or fewer persons all in one room or area seem to work best, but dividing large groups into smaller groups often does not work. Two or more groups in the same space working at the same task are also difficult to manage.

Interest Groups. In this style of grouping, several different types of activities are presented simultaneously. Campers are then asked to move around to determine for themselves which activity they want to participate in. Parents and leaders are encouraged to allow children to make their own decisions and not to hold to any kind of family structure. With this style of grouping, it is most helpful to have the initial selection period in one large room or area because movement from one interest area to another does not happen easily when several rooms are used, particularly if they are remote from one another.

Activity Groups. These are organized with four to ten campers in each, for predetermined activities. In some cases, all the activity groups may be participating in similar tasks. But at other times the assigned activities may be totally different, although relating to the same theme. The chief difference between an activity group and an interest group is the freedom of choice of interest groups. Activity groups can be organized by (1) dividing the total group into age groups, (2) counting off to form equal-sized groups, (3) drawing straws, or (4) using a common denominator, such as months of birth.

Family Groups. In this style of grouping, all campers of a family unit work together. This is a fairly easy way to organize groups, and is especially useful when your goal is to strengthen relationships within the family, but I must caution you that single persons and members of single-parent families may feel left out with this style of grouping.

Restructured Family Groups. No two members of the same biological family work together in this style of grouping, but new "families" are formed. Camp leaders will appreciate preregistration for this style of grouping, but it is possible to make last-minute adjustments. Single adults can easily be included, and individual campers can be assigned family roles within the new "family," such as father, grandmother, aunt, or cousin. This style is perhaps too complicated for a one-time event if small children are involved, because they seem to adapt slowly to the new groups.

Family Clusters. In this type of grouping, as many as four biological families participate together as a unit. This style does work well for a one-time event.

MAINSTREAMING CAMPERS
WHO HAVE DISABILITIES

There is still one group to consider, which for the most part has additional characteristics and concerns: potential campers who must contend with handicapping conditions. Many camps exclude them, some provide a special session just for "special campers," and a few camps have the joy (yes, and the heartaches) of "mainstreaming" those individuals throughout the camping year. By mainstreaming I mean including one or two persons who have disabling conditions in each cabin group, and welcoming them to participate as they are able in all the regular camp activities. In some cases you may have to assign an extra staff person to be with the group at times to provide any special assistance needed, especially so that the counselor does not get completely worn out. In our case, handicapped campers make up about 8 percent of our total camper population. We have had excellent results, too, in employing mentally and physically handicapped staff members, for kitchen and maintenance work and also, in one case, as a cabin counselor. (In the latter case we also employed an attendant for the counselor, who was confined to a wheelchair, and it was beautiful to watch a deep relationship develop between them over the summer.)

Developing positive relationships is really "the name of the game" in intergenerational programming as in all camp settings. And when handicapped campers are mainstreamed with "typical" campers, all can begin to learn who they are and what they have to share: gratitude for being included, affection for God's family, and new insights, because as persons, even with minds or bodies not fully usable, they still see and share creation in their own special ways.

PART ONE:
Planning an Intergenerational Camp Program

2.
Elements of Planning

Planning for an intergenerational camp on the theme of the stewardship of creation will be slightly different from planning a camping experience, even on the same theme, for a homogeneous age group. You will be working to involve participants from a number of generations in a way that may not have been explored in your camp setting before. In addition, the study theme probably is not one with which campers or staff have dealt in a large group before, although it is an area that probably has been considered by most of the adults. They will bring with them a considerable background of information, experiences, and concerns.

WHO WILL DO THE PLANNING?

This book has been written with several groups of readers in mind, all of whom have important roles in the planning process.

1. The first group I have in mind are persons who serve as full-time camp program directors, or who serve on a program committee, at established camps that provide eight or more weeks of Bible camp every summer and that may employ college-age persons as counselors.

2. Next, I have in mind persons who will be serving as deans of a one-week church camp program, perhaps at a rented facility, often directing a volunteer staff of counselors, and working with a year-round staff of the facility.

3. Definitely, I am writing for the counselors who will have the direct responsibility of living with the campers and leading daily Bible studies and other program activities for a week or more.

4. Finally, some readers will be leading weekend retreats.

It will be apparent to you as you read that some of the planning material may not apply to you and the group with whom you are preparing to work. However, it can give you an idea of the planning that has gone on, or that will go on, as a wide variety of individuals get ready for camp.

There are certain basics in planning for a church camp that are the same no matter what the theme or the age range of the participants: setting goals and objectives, determining available resources, planning how to use them, planning the day-by-day program, and evaluating. If you are new to church camp planning, I suggest that you read Ted R. Witt's *Responsible with Creation* or Don Griggs's *Teaching Teachers to Teach* to help you with the planning process. To assist in planning for the intergenerational approach, I recommend Paul and Barbara Kehnle's *Intergenerational Camping* and Marguerite R. Berssert's *Intergenerational Manual for Christian Education: Shared Approaches*.

You will need to do your own personal planning, and then some extensive planning with your coleaders, with the camp management, and finally with the participants themselves.

Planning should begin several months at least before the actual camp experience is to begin. In our programs we start theme preparation in October for the following June and even then sometimes feel rushed!

Of course, one of the first things that should be done is to select the site for the camp experience. Visit the camp. Check on costs, staff of the facility, privacy factors, available equipment, comfort capabilities, meal schedules (and sample menus), emergency plans, and what you need to provide. Get a contract in writing!

Personal Planning

Before you begin to plan with others, you should read through the thematic materials yourself and get in touch with your own attitudes about the stewardship of creation. Where are your values and priorities? How does your present life-style reflect your personal "theology of ecology"? What areas would you like to try to change? What areas would you like to reinforce? What ideas in the materials interest you the most as you look forward to working with an intergenerational group at camp? With whom would you like to work on the staff? What special opportunities offered by this particular camp are available to you? Begin to select the program activities that interest you the most.

As you read this book, use your Bible (I suggest Today's English Version, the Good News Bible) to look up Scriptural references and reflect on what they have to say to you now. What does "stewardship" mean to you? What is included in "creation"? What is your vision of the stewardship of creation? How has this changed in the past several years? What sorts of changes are you being called to make?

After you have considered the theme materials yourself, you will be ready to move on to planning for a larger group experience in shared learning. First of all, you must consider for whom you are planning and where you fit into the overall plan. As you prepare for your experience, please be sure to refer to the separate age level guides, which supplement the materials presented in this resource book. If you are working with children (ages 8–11), younger youth (12–14), or older youth (15–18), it is especially important to consult the correct age level guide.

Planning with Coleaders

As soon as you know who the other leaders are with whom you will be working in your intergenerational program, you will want to meet and get acquainted. Plan to worship together as part of your planning process. Share with one another where you are in your own lives in regard to the stewardship of creation. Share the stories of your lives so that you will come to appreciate each other's strengths and abilities. Determine who is going to be responsible for which parts of the program and which activities. Put it down in writing and give each person a copy of the list so there are no misunderstandings. Settle some very practical matters: Who is responsible for relationships with the camp facility director/manager? (Be sure to direct all communication to the resident camp staff through one individual!) Who will be responsible for publicity? Who will register the campers and make cabin assignments? Who will enlist additional staff (voluntary and otherwise)? Who will be responsible for transportation? Who will purchase any needed materials or equipment? Who will be responsible for discipline? Who handles the money? And so forth. Be sure to spend enough time with your coleaders to become comfortable with one another and begin to feel a sense of being part of a team.

Next, you will want to set goals and objectives for your intergenerational camping experience. Goals are the broader directions you would like to set for your group, and objectives are the specific, measurable, achievable guidelines for reaching your desired goal. Without goals and objectives you may find yourself floundering, not knowing where you want to go. Setting goals and objectives for the group (and agreeing on them) helps you to determine more easily the specific activities you will select to reach your desired outcomes. They will help all of you to work together as a team and will let you know when you have accomplished what you set out to do. Setting realistic goals and measurable objectives will help you avoid a lot of frustrations, too!

After you have set goals and objectives, list all the activities you can that might deal with the theme. A number are included in this resource, and you and your coleaders can think of many more. Remember, it is all right to make up a new activity or to modify an old one—that's part of being a cocreator! Brainstorm other possible resources and resource people. For example, does your denomination publish special materials on world hunger that you can secure in quantities to pass out to campers? Does your local utility company have printed information on the conservation of energy? Which organizations can you contact to secure films or literature on peace or justice concerns? Who in your congregation is particularly knowledgeable about gardening or fitness and might be willing to share with the group? List several options for each of the scheduled program units each day. It is a good idea to provide a number of options from which participants can choose. Structure each day so that there are activities planned for both the intergenerational group and the individual age groups.

Planning with the Camp Management

A camp is an ideal environment for learning about, and recommitting ourselves to, our stewardship of creation. It is possible, however, that while the director/manager may wholeheartedly agree with your basic philosophy and probably will be eager to work with you, the existing camp facilities may not reflect a deep sensitivity to ecology and energy conservation. Many church camps were built in the days when energy sources seemed to be inexhaustible, and the types of construction used show this. By the same token, most camps were originally just for children in the warm summer months. Since no one was expected to use the facilities at other times of the year, no one considered insulation or weathertight construction. I would venture to guess that the camp director/manager already knows in general where the facilities are lacking and will be happy for whatever help you can give to "weatherize" the camp and cut costs.

So, early in your planning, you and your coleaders should visit the camp and meet with the resident staff. Tell them what you want to accomplish and elicit their cooperation and ideas. Look for evidence that the camp staff is sensitive to conservation, ecology, and simple living, and be appreciative of whatever attempts they have made to honor these values in the environment. For example, is there a garden? In what ways can it be used in your program? Is the dining hall menu wholesome? Can you work with the cook to design some teaching experiences around the food that will be served? Does the camp staff already encourage campers to share in the tasks of running the camp? Will the staff assist in planning, assigning, and leading meaningful daily chore-time activities?

If you find the campsite less than ideal, look for places you and your campers can make slight modifications that will benefit everyone. Negotiate for what is possible, and push gently where appropriate. Agreeing that the camp canteen will be stocked with only nutritious and wholesome snacks instead of the typical junk food may seem like a small victory, but it is a place to begin! Perhaps you can offer to build a compost bin, which will remain long after you are gone.

Next, survey the site for its unique natural features, such as a lake, waterfall, mountain, forest, meadow, or stream. Consider the man-made features, especially those of former days. Most campsites were used for something else before they became church camps—farms, mining villages, lumberjack camps, fishing camps, or wilderness. What evidence do you see of the previous occupants? How can you utilize these natural and man-made features to full advantage in your daily activities? Think in terms of Bible study, theme exploration and discussion, recreation, and worship.

Another consideration is the space that is available for different-sized groups. Where can you assemble all your participants at one time, indoors and outdoors? Are there safe and suitable places for younger children while adults are engaged in separate activities? You will need to match the kinds of activities you want to do with the space available.

The camp director/manager will also be able to tell you what resource people, programs, and equipment can be provided by the camp. If the resident staff includes a nurse, lifeguard, crafts leader, or naturalist, for example, you can perhaps use these persons to supplement your own staff. Here is a word of caution: do not assume, just because the camp is on a lake, for example, and has a dock and boats, that you can use them without additional cost. We routinely use a camp all summer where we even have to provide the toilet tissue. The point: make sure you know what is provided by whom before you get to camp and are surprised!

Planning with Participants

A wise person once said, "All of us know more than any one of us!" Believing this fully, I want to urge you strongly to do your final planning with the participants at camp. After the session has actually begun, when the people have gotten a bit acquainted with the site, one another, and your leaders, then get together for your final planning with them. You can lay out the overall time schedule for the week (or whatever period you are spending together) and suggest options from which they can choose.

One way to accomplish this is to have a "town meeting" with everyone present. Using a large master schedule sheet, have the campers fill in what they would like to do together, being conscious that there must be private, small-group, and large-group time every day. You will want to give participants a time to share their expectations for camp and to give them "ownership" for fulfilling these expectations by having them choose how they will spend their time.

It is likely that the participants will have various levels of expertise related to the theme that would be appropriate to share with the rest of the group. For example, you may have a geological engineer who can tell you how to stabilize a slope or when and where to use six-legged tetrahedrons (a fairly new method of preventing bank erosion along flooding rivers), a 4–H student who can give practical advice on keeping down offensive odors in pigpens or compost bins, a housewife who has extensive and correct knowledge of the dangers of nuclear energy production, and a child who can share the proper method of sorting out items for recycling. The town meeting will give them all a chance to offer to share their skills, knowledge, and ideas. A daily town meeting will provide even more opportunities for people to volunteer to share. Be sure to actively encourage contributions from the youngest participants too.

SAMPLE SCHEDULE FOR A WEEK-LONG CAMP

The following sample schedule is presented as a guide. There is enough flexibility so that the various time slots can be used in various ways depending on the needs and desires of the participants. During the planning periods with the campers, you can determine where their interests lie and then "plug in" more activities from that area of concern. Other factors, such as the weather, the availability of some outside resource persons, or a nearby event that is open to the public, should also be taken into consideration. Do not let the schedule run you! Stay loose, and be open to whatever opportunities God presents.

DAY 1 (Usually Sunday)

2–4 P.M.: Campers arrive; register; are assigned to housing; settle in

4 P.M.: Total camp gathering; introduce program staff; briefly explain camp rules and the schedule for remainder of day

4:30 P.M.: Brief get-acquainted tour of camp in small groups (point out nurse's station, dining hall, fire alarm system, chapel, campfire area, canteen, craft area, and so forth)

6 P.M.: Dinner; welcome from site director/manager

7:30 P.M.: Get-acquainted activities to meet others and to divide into some of the various small groups for the week

8:30 P.M.: Campfire with devotional message on theme (see page 22)

9:15 P.M.: Refreshments; informal get-acquainted period; small children to bed

10 P.M.: Closing prayer

DAY 2 (Monday)

7:45 A.M.: Morning watch (see Chapter 3, "Worship and Bible Study Suggestions")

8 A.M.: Breakfast

8:45 A.M.: Cabin cleanup

9:15 A.M.: Tioshpa (reportedly a native American term that means "the gathering of the family." In an intergenerational setting in which we are trying to operate as the family of God, *tioshpa* is an appropriate name for our morning devotions). Include an inspirational meditation on the theme of "The Original Agreement" (see Chapter 4)

9:45 A.M.: Bible study on "The Vision of God's Shalom" (see Chapter 3)

10:30 A.M.: Coffee break

10:45 A.M.: Group study on "The Gift of Land" (see first two thirds of Chapter 7, "The Gift of Land and Water")

11:45 A.M.: Chore time

12:30 P.M.: Lunch; explain fire-drill procedures

1:15 P.M.: Quiet time for rest and personal reflection

2 P.M.: Fire drill

2:30 P.M.: Free time for optional activities: swimming, crafts, games, and so forth

4:30 P.M.: Family (small group) time for junk hike and art from junk craft (see Chapter 7)

6 P.M.: Dinner

7:30 P.M.: Group singing

8 P.M.: Intergenerational session: Memory event (see Appendix)

9 P.M.: Campfire

9:30 P.M.: Adult activities—youngsters to bed

10 P.M.: Closing prayer

DAY 3 (Tuesday)

7:45 A.M. Morning watch (see Chapter 3)

8 A.M.: Breakfast

8:45 A.M.: Cabin cleanup

9:15 A.M.: Tioshpa, with meditation on "The Broken Agreement" (see Chapter 5)

9:45 A.M.: Bible study on "The Roots of the Problem" (see Chapter 3)

10:30 A.M.: Coffee break

10:45 A.M.: Group study on water (see last third of Chapter 7)

11:45 A.M.: Chore time

12:30 P.M.: Lunch

1:15 P.M.: Quiet time

2 P.M.: Free time for optional activities and projects

4:30 P.M.: Family (small group) time to discuss and plan possible projects at home

6 P.M.: Dinner

7:30 P.M.: Group singing

8 P.M.: Program session: intergenerational movie and discussion on theme

9 P.M.: Campfire with devotional message on theme

9:30 P.M.: Adult activities of their choice—youngsters to bed

10 P.M.: Closing prayer

DAY 4 (Wednesday)

7:45 A.M.: Morning watch (see Chapter 3)

8 A.M.: Breakfast

8:45 A.M.: Cabin cleanup

9:15 A.M.: Tioshpa on "The Task for Us Now" (see Chapter 6)

9:45 A.M.: Bible study on "The Roots of Our Faith" (see Chapter 3)

10:30 A.M.: Coffee break

10:45 A.M.: Group study on "Food" and kitchen tour (see Chapter 8)

11:45 A.M.: Chore time

12:30 P.M.: Lunch

1:15 P.M.: Quiet time

2 P.M.: Camp olympics, followed by free time for optional activities

4:30 P.M.: Family (small group) time—food montage or visual display (see Chapter 8)

6 P.M.: Dinner—perhaps a simulation on world hunger

7:30 P.M.: Group singing

8 P.M.: Program session—intergenerational "time machine" (see Appendix)

9 P.M.: Campfire; devotional message

9:30 P.M.: Adult activities of their choice—youngsters to bed

10 P.M.: Closing prayer

DAY 5 (Thursday)

7:45 A.M.: Morning watch (see Chapter 3)

8 A.M.: Breakfast

8:45 A.M.: Cabin cleanup

9:15 A.M.: Tioshpa on "Healthful Wholeness" (see Chapter 9)

9:45 A.M.: Bible study on "Planting Seeds" (see Chapter 3)

10:30 A.M.: Coffee break

10:45 A.M.: Group time—energy discussion and camp tour to discover ways to conserve energy (also view solar-/wind-/water-powered equipment) (see Chapter 10)

11:45 A.M.: Chore time

12:30 P.M.: Lunch

1:15 P.M.: Quiet time

2 P.M.: Free time for optional activities

4:30 P.M.: Family (small group) time to discuss and plan how to conserve energy at home and/or how to promote family wellness

6 P.M.: Dinner

7:30 P.M.: Group singing

8 P.M.: Program session—movie on energy conservation

9 P.M.: Campfire with devotional message on day's theme

9:30 P.M.: Adult activities of their choice—youngsters to bed

10 P.M.: Closing prayer

DAY 6 (Friday)

7:45 A.M.: Morning watch (see Chapter 3)

8 A.M.: Breakfast

8:45 A.M.: Cabin cleanup

9:15 A.M.: Tioshpa on "Peace and Justice" (see Chapter 11)

9:45 A.M.: Bible study on "The Feast of Faith" (see Chapter 3)

10:30 A.M.: Coffee break

10:45 A.M.: Group time to discuss "just war concept" (see Chapter 11), study denominational statement on conscientious objection, and study models (see Appendix)

11:45 A.M.: Chore time

12:30 P.M.: Lunch

1:15 P.M.: Quiet time

2 P.M.: Free time for optional activities

4:30 P.M.: Family (small group) time to write a group statement (see Chapter 11) and to discuss and plan steps to be taken at home to promote peace and justice (see Appendix, page 91)

6 P.M.: Dinner

7:30 P.M.: Group singing

8 P.M.: Family (small group) time to discuss week at camp, with emphasis on how to rededicate ourselves to working for God's vision of Shalom

9 P.M.: Campfire with devotional meditation on rededication to the stewardship of creation (God's Shalom vision)

9:30 P.M.: Adult sharing time—youngsters to bed

10 P.M.: Closing prayer

DAY 7 (Saturday)

7:45 A.M.: Same as Day 2

8 A.M.: Breakfast

8:45 A.M.: Cabin cleanup and "camp sweep"

10 A.M.: Service of dedication and commitment (see Appendix)

11 A.M.: Leave for home

INTERGENERATIONAL RETREAT

A retreat is a planned, church-sponsored spiritual experience. It is a way of going beyond knowing about the truths of faith to experiencing them. A retreat is a small-group experience of devotion, withdrawal, fellowship, and sharing in the company of God and other persons. It is an experience of intentional living together in a special pattern of spiritual discipline as preparation for a renewed Christian ministry of witness and service to the world.

Planning Your Retreat

Select a retreat committee of three to five persons who, ideally, have had the experience of retreat. This committee answers the following questions:

1. Why are we going to have a retreat? What is its purpose?

2. Where will the retreat be held? Check on cost, staff of the facility, privacy factors, equipment, comfort capabilities, and meal schedule. Reserve your retreat dates as far in advance as possible (most good retreat centers fill up their schedules rapidly) and get a contract in writing.

3. What will we do on our retreat? What is our time schedule? Be sure to include free time for retreatants to relax, engage in conversation, or enjoy private periods of silence and meditation.

4. Who will lead the retreat? The leaders should meet with the committee so they will understand the intent, schedule, and details of the retreat.

5. Who will come to the retreat? Invite participation through posters, letters, phone calls, and personal contact.

6. After the experience of this retreat, do we want to have another? Prepare an evaluation form to be completed a week or so after the retreat to give retreatants an opportunity to think over the experience amidst the events of daily life.

Some Reminders as You Prepare for Retreat

The basic qualification for a retreatant is to come as you are, but with a desire to be different, to be better, to be more like the steward of creation that God offers to make you through infinite grace.

In retreat there is no group of the "attained" trying to "bring others across." All, including the resource persons, are participants, part of the fellowship of need, of seeking minds and open hearts.

Come expecting periods of silence, not only when you are alone, but when you are in the group. The discipline of silence, properly experienced, offers opportunity for listening to God and responding.

Look forward to discussions that are informed by study of the Word of God, strengthened by honesty, and tempered by grace in a climate in which defensiveness, ridicule, self-projection, and pride are reduced.

If this is your first retreat experience, come with an open mind. Ask God to be your teacher. The winds of change may be the breath of the Holy Spirit offering you new life and power!

A Sample Schedule for an Intergenerational Retreat

FRIDAY

7–8 P.M.: Arrival and settling in; name tags and some get-acquainted activities should be set up for people as they arrive

8 P.M.: Opening prayer; discussion of goals; contracting session; explanation of weekend schedule and rules; introduce leaders and facility staff

8:30 P.M.: Movie on theme to set focus of retreat

9 P.M.: Refreshments; younger children to bed

9:15 P.M.: Small groups meet to discuss various aspects of theme

10 P.M.: Closing prayer

SATURDAY

7:45 A.M.: Morning watch in family groups

8 A.M.: Breakfast

8:45 A.M.: Cabin cleanup

9:15 A.M.: Tioshpa ("gathering of the family") with brief meditation on theme of stewardship

9:45 A.M.: Sign-up for various activities, projects

10:15 A.M.: Coffee break

10:45 A.M.: Intergenerational Bible study on theme

12 NOON: Lunch

1 P.M.: Quiet time

2 P.M.: Optional activities, projects, hikes, games, swimming

4 P.M.: Interest groups No. 1—sharing time on various stewardship subjects

5 P.M.: Interest groups No. 2—sharing time on various stewardship subjects

6 P.M.: Dinner with simulation on world hunger, if possible

7 P.M.: Total group game

8 P.M.: Separate age groups on theme "What Can We Do?"

8:45 P.M.: Total group assembles to hear brief reports from previous session

9 P.M.: Campfire (or vespers) with devotional meditation on theme

9:30 P.M.: Refreshments

10 P.M.: Closing prayer

SUNDAY

7:45 A.M.: Morning watch

8 A.M.: Breakfast

8:45 A.M.: Cabin cleanup

9:15 A.M.: Small groups plan worship—include the children!

11 A.M.: Closing worship celebration

3.
Worship and Bible Study Suggestions

DEVOTIONS FOR THE FIRST EVENING IN CAMP

The first evening of the camp week sets the tone for all that follows. It is important, therefore, to offer a meaningful, well-thought-out but brief devotional service during that time. It can be quite informal. As the campers gather, join together in singing some fairly well-known songs. The leader can briefly tell about the worship and Bible study opportunities for the week and explain the theme. Ask for prayer requests, and then include them in the evening prayers. Close with one or two favorite hymns.

Seed Thoughts for the Evening Meditation

God is love, and God calls on you and me to love one another—not just those at camp with us, not just those back home, but all of God's creation everywhere. And God also calls on us to be faithful stewards, to care for God's creation. This week we will remember our Christian heritage as we consider God's Word and as we pray some prayers first prayed by earlier followers of Jesus. We will look at some of the major problems facing people around the world, and we will consider what part each of us can play in restoring the balance originally set by God. And we will talk a lot about God's will for Shalom, the Biblical word for peace, which includes total well-being, wholeness, fulfillment, health, and joyous harmony. In *Isa., ch. 2,* God calls on us to turn our swords into plowshares and our spears into pruning hooks. To accomplish that nationally and internationally will be a big job because weapons of war and implements of agriculture imply totally different life-styles. At times we may wonder what we as individuals can do. But because we want to be faithful stewards, and because we remember that a journey of a thousand miles begins with just one step, we will rededicate ourselves to be a part of God's solution.

MORNING WATCH

Morning watch plays an important role in the day at camp. It offers a period for personal reflection, and allows campers some private thinking time, usually scheduled for early in the day. In an intergenerational setting, it is suggested that family groups spend the time together.

Many of us need some structure to guide our reflections. We need things to think about. The following morning watch suggestions can be reproduced in quantity for each day and given to the campers as they go off for morning watch.

Initially you may need to explain the purpose and value of morning watch. You should also tell them that the prayer suggestions are from the ancient Christian church and are included to help us understand the bond with our heritage of faith.

Day 2—Isa. 2:2-3 (Monday)

To think about—Coming to camp is like going up the hill of the Lord. What three things can I do each day to walk in the path God has chosen for me?

Prayer—"O God Almighty, Father of our Lord Jesus Christ, give me a body unstained by the world, a heart that is pure in its love for you and your children, a mind that is watchful for ways I can help others, and the presence of your Holy Spirit so that I can hold fast to an unshaken faith in your truth. In Jesus' name. Amen." (The Clementine Liturgy, first century, adapted)

Day 3—James 3:13-18 (Tuesday)

To think about—God has promised to give us wisdom that is pure, peaceful, gentle, and friendly. In what five ways today can I express my friendliness to others, and how can I change the way I live to be more gentle with the earth and its creatures?

Prayer—"Grant your servants, O God, to be set on fire with your Holy Spirit, strengthened by your power, illuminated by your splendor, filled with your grace, so we can go on with your aid. Give us today a right faith, perfect love for one another, and true humility. Fill our lives with simple affection, brave patience, persevering obedience, and perpetual peace. In Jesus' name. Amen." (Old Gallican Sacramentary, third century, adapted)

Day 4—Heb. 13:20-21 (Wednesday)

To think about—Scriptures tell us that God has already provided us with everything we need to do the Lord's will. What special gifts have I received and how can I use them for God and humankind?

Prayer—"Most high God, infinite in majesty, I call upon you today for all your servants everywhere, that you will give us pure minds, perfect love, sincerity in conduct, purity in heart, strength in action, courage in distress, and self-command in character. Give us the grace of devotion to your will, fulfill our desires with good gifts, and crown us with your mercy so we can praise you forever and ever. In Jesus' name. Amen." (Gallican Sacramentary, fourth century, adapted)

Day 5—Col. 1:15-22 (Thursday)

To think about—In this passage Paul writes about the restoration of the whole creation. God is not a God of destruction, abandonment, or death, but the God of life, peace, and joy. In what ways can my family and I start to respond to God's call to be peacemakers in a warring world and to take better care of the world we have been given dominion over?

Prayer—"O Lord, our Savior, who have warned us that you will expect much from those to whom much has been given: Grant today that we who have so many of this world's blessings may work together more abundantly to extend to others what we so richly enjoy, in fulfillment of your holy will; through Jesus Christ our Lord. Amen." (Augustine, fourth century, adapted)

Day 6—Matt. 10:34-39 (Friday)

To think about—Christ did not come to give peace as the world gives peace, but to declare war on the world's unjust peace. Being on Christ's side means taking risks. When I return home how can I continue my efforts to be a good steward of all God's creation, and how can I enlist and encourage others to join in this effort?

Prayer—"O God, from whom all holy desires, all good counsels, and all just works do proceed: Give unto your servants that peace which the world cannot give, that our hearts may be set to obey your commandments, and also that we, being defended from the fear of our enemies, may pass our time in rest and quietness. We commit ourselves into your hands, O God, and ask for your aid in knowing your will so that we can follow it perfectly and gladly, to the honor and glory of your name; through Jesus Christ our Lord. Amen." (Gelasian Sacramentary, fifth century, adapted)

Day 7—Matt. 22:34-40 (Saturday)

To think about—In a short time we will be leaving camp and returning home. In the moments remaining, how can I express my love to the others in my group? Do I have their names and addresses so I can keep in touch and encourage them to be faithful stewards? What are the first three things I am going to do to change my life-style when I get home?

Prayer—

"Lord, make me an instrument of your peace;
Where there is hate, let me bring love;
Where there is malice, forgiveness;
Where there are disputes, reconciliation;
Where there is error, truth;
Where there is doubt, belief;
Where there is despair, hope;
Where there is darkness, your light;
Where there is sorrow, joy!
O Master, let me strive more to comfort others than to be comforted,
To understand others than to be understood,
To love others than to be loved!
For the person who gives, receives;
The person who forgives, receives forgiveness;
And dying, we rise again to eternal life. Amen."
(Francis of Assisi, thirteenth century, adapted)

DAILY BIBLE STUDY STYLES

The daily study of Scripture is one of the most vital aspects of the church camp program, and preparation for these small-group periods deserves your prayerful attention. In fact, prayer is so basic to Bible study that the group should begin and end each daily session with prayer, asking for the presence of the Holy Spirit. There are many ways to conduct a Bible study, and you may already have a favorite method, or the camp program director may specify a method you are to use. I want to suggest two different methods you can try. You may find it useful to vary your method from day to day.

Inductive Bible Study

Do. The group does something together. This may be an experience, such as a visit to a nearby nursing home or a soup kitchen. Maybe you went on a hike to observe the problems involved in soil erosion. Whatever it is, the group has done something other than Bible study and they want to understand it better.

Reflect. During this step, the group reflects on what has happened, what they saw, or what they have discussed. Key questions from the counselor will guide their reflection: How did you feel? What does that mean? How does this relate to you?

Analyze. At this point you turn to the Bible and select a text that will help the group analyze what they have experienced. In the Bible studies that follow, you will have to consider the daily theme and the suggested passages before you decide what experience to plan for the group to reflect on. Then ask, How do these passages help us understand what we saw, or what we did, or what is happening to us?

Generalize. After the group has reflected on and analyzed its experience, the members can draw some general conclusions. Ask them, What implications do these passages have for the way we live our lives?

Deductive Bible Study

The deductive method of Bible study differs from the inductive method in that the group begins with the Bible and then group members reflect on their life experiences. The basic method has six steps.

Read. It is important that all members of the group read the passages to be considered. In an intergenerational setting, it may be necessary to have some member of the group read the passage aloud slowly and thoughtfully.

Reflect. Each member of the group reflects on the passage, trying to dig out its meaning for his or her life. The counselor can guide this reflection by asking, What are the key points of this passage for you?

Share. After a brief period of reflection, members of the group are invited to share their various individual insights and, in discussion, to help sort these out to find some common understandings.

Explore. Next, the group tries to discover what this passage meant to the original readers. This requires some exploration of background, history, and perhaps literary analysis. It is good to have several commentaries available for the group to use, or at least the counselor should have become knowledgeable in this area. Sometimes this step reveals that modern-day individual insights do not help us understand the original meaning properly.

Apply. Next, the counselor helps members of the group bring the passage to bear on their own daily lives by asking questions such as, What does this mean for your life? What is it that God is telling you to do?

Express. It helps translate Bible study into life if we can express what we have learned. Suitable techniques include role-playing, making a collage, drawing a poster, or rewriting the passage in our own words. These expressive activities should be shared and discussed.

DAILY BIBLE STUDIES

Day 2—Theme: God's Shalom Vision (Monday)

Objectives: To help campers accept a holistic view of creation in which God is central and all parts are interrelated and interdependent; and to encourage campers to adopt the Shalom vision as their own for the world around us.

Bible passages to consider: *Gen. 1:1 to 2:4a; Ps. 37:1-11; Ps. 85:4-13; Zech. 8:9-12; Job, ch. 38; Col. 1:15-23.*

Day 3—Theme: Roots of the Problem (Tuesday)

Objectives: To increase campers' awareness concerning root causes of hunger, poverty, illness, injustice, energy shortages, and lack of peace; and to help campers understand how our use of natural resources affects our brothers and sisters around the world.

Bible passages to consider: *Ex. 20:1-17; Jer. 6:9-15; Ezek. 13:1-6; Ezek., ch. 34; I Cor. 12:26; I Tim. 6:10.*

Day 4—Theme: The Roots of Our Faith (Wednesday)

Objectives: To help campers discover their roots of faith; to identify our bond with our heritage; and to put the Shalom vision to work in our everyday lives.

Bible passages to consider: *Deut. 26:1-10; Micah 6:8; Rom. 8:31-39; I Cor. 1:10; Eph. 4:1-6; Heb. 11:1 to 12:2.*

Day 5—Theme: Planting Seeds (Thursday)

Objectives: To assist campers to determine to modify their life-styles toward a simpler pattern of consumption; and to provide models for a simpler life.

Bible passages to consider: *Ps. 72:1-4; Prov. 31:8-9; Matt. 13:3b-9; Luke 19:8; Phil. 2:3-5; I Tim. 4:4; I John 3:17-18.*

Day 6—Theme: The Feast of Faith (Friday)

Objectives: To assist campers to establish a plan of action that can be followed at home in working with fellow Christians and other organizations toward Shalom (peace); and to dedicate ourselves and our possessions to work for peace because we have the vision of God's Shalom.

Bible passages to consider: *Deut. 15:7-11; II Sam. 12:1-15; Isa. 2:1-4; John 14:15-31; Rom. 14:13-19; II Cor. 5:11-21.*

PART TWO: Reflection on the Theme— Stewardship of Creation

4.
The Original Agreement

"In the beginning . . . God created the universe." *(Gen. 1:1.)* That is a good place to start our study of "The Stewardship of Creation." We will ask three questions: What was the original agreement? Between whom was the agreement made? How does that agreement apply to us today?

When the universe was fashioned and our earth was born, there was a plan, a purpose, a direction. Behind it all is the Creator, Almighty God, who has the power to form all of creation out of nothingness!

The universe in which we live has the stamp of quality on it. Nothing created by God is evil in itself. All of creation is good. Down through the years, however, some members of the Christian family have misunderstood the creation's goodness. Examples of this are seen in the monastic movement's stress on separation from the world and the pietistic tendency to identify evil with things rather than with the misuse of things. Yet, although creation is good, we recognize that all the good things God created must have divine controls on them, and they must be used in the divinely intended way.

So a paradise awaited Adam and Eve who, created in God's image, were given a garden home that could fulfill their every need. God said, "I have provided all kinds of grain and all kinds of fruit for you to eat." *(Gen. 1:29.)* Clearly, God created the world in terms of God's children's needs, and then when all was ready, God gave the earth to humankind to care for.

No part of creation takes on more importance in God's eyes than humanity. We are the very crown of the whole creative process on earth—the chief object of God's saving love. In the beginning the power of creation belonged to God alone. But very soon God sought to share this power with us, and we were called on to participate in an ongoing creative venture. Life must bring forth life. God blessed us and said, "Have many children, so that your descendants will live all over the earth and bring it under their control." *(Gen. 1:28.)*

What do these words mean? Some people have understood them to be a license to exploit the earth and its resources. We will talk more of this later when we look at the condition we find ourselves in today. The fact is that God is still the creator/owner. You and I may possess legal rights to a plot of ground. We may use every good gift God has provided. But nothing within the framework of God's agreement permits us to say of any given thing, "It is mine." The earth and all things on it, including you and me, belong to God! We are not our own. We are owned!

God made an agreement with Adam and Eve and all their descendants, which includes you and me. In the agreement God said, "Have many children, so that your descendants will live all over the earth and bring it under their control. I am putting you in charge of the fish, the birds, and all the wild animals." *(Gen. 1:28.)*

The key phrase here is "bring it under their control." In Hebrew this is expressed with the verb *redah*. What does this word mean? Two Old Testament texts give us positive and negative definitions. The positive example is found in *Ps. 72*, which is a prayer at the coronation of a new king. The psalm describes what the king's rule should be like:

> Teach the king to judge with your righteousness, O God;
>   share with him your own justice,
> so that he will rule over your people with justice
>   and govern the oppressed with righteousness. . . .
> May the king judge the poor fairly;
>   may he help the needy
>   and defeat their oppressors. . . .
> He has pity on the weak and poor;
>   he saves the lives of those in need.

(Ps. 72:1–2, 4, 13.)

If you read through the entire psalm, you will get a picture of an ideal king. He will have a special concern for the weak, the powerless, and the helpless. For a king to "have control" or "be in charge" does not mean to rob or exploit the people over whom he rules. Quite the opposite—the idea is to protect and care for his subjects, with special attention to the weak and helpless.

The negative example is provided by the prophet Ezekiel, who points out the lack of care provided by the kings of Israel. He says, "You are doomed, you shepherds of Israel! You take care of yourselves, but never tend the sheep. You drink the milk, wear clothes made from the wool, and kill and eat the finest sheep. But you never tend the sheep. You have not taken care of the weak ones, healed the ones that are sick, bandaged the ones that are hurt, brought back the ones that wandered off, or looked for the ones that were lost. Instead, you treated them cruelly." *(Ezek. 34:2b-4.)*

So the gift of the earth does not confer ownership. Rather the people are free to use, enjoy, and benefit from the land, but not to possess, abuse, or destroy it. We are to serve as God's stewards of what continues to be God's. The promise is that as we take care of the land, the land will take care of us. In today's language we would say that good earth-care practices require us to take no more than that which can and will be replenished. That is the agreement made in the beginning between God and humanity, an agreement that is still in effect today with us.

Interestingly enough, the agreement to be good stewards of the earth comes to us not only from the Hebrew Scriptures. Perhaps the clearest example from another culture is contained in the basic teachings of the American Indian. Simply stated, the native American still teaches that the earth is a gift from a gracious Creator, that all life comes from the earth, that all our needs can be met by tribal and not private control of the land, and that renewability of the land and its resources is the stewardship responsibility of all human beings. In *Rom. 2:15,* Paul said, "Their conduct shows that what the Law commands is written in their hearts." Certainly, much of the native American attitude toward the land demonstrates that Almighty God has written into the hearts of all human beings a vision of order and justice.

5.
The Broken Agreement

According to the first chapter of the Bible, the first words God spoke to the first human being were words that have to do with the stewardship of creation. Or, to say it in a more modern way, the first thought God communicated to human beings dealt with environmental protection. Genesis tells us that one reason God created human beings was that, up to the time of our formation, "there was no one to cultivate the land" *(Gen. 2:5).* The agreement was that God would share creative powers with humans for all time, whereas our part is to be honest stewards of God's earth and all that goes with it. We have been put in charge to be good managers!

It was not long, however, before Adam and Eve broke the agreement. For their willful disobedience they were sent out of the Garden of Eden. But though the Lord told them, "You will have to work hard all your life to make [the ground] produce enough food for you" *(Gen. 3:17),* the stewardship responsibility was still there—they were still supposed to be in charge.

Down through the years their descendants, even to our generation, have continued in their footsteps and have broken the agreement. Time after time God has brought us back and reaffirmed our role as the stewards of creation. But in spite of God's faithfulness, and in spite of nearly two thousand years of having heard and accepted the good news of Jesus Christ, even we Christians continue, for the most part, to break our side of the agreement. We can see this all around us.

Possibly the clearest picture we have of our lack of stewardship was presented in 1980 in the document entitled *The Global 2000 Report to the President,* which is part of the U.S. Government's effort to do something about the growing awareness of the interdependence of population, resources, and environment.

The *Global 2000 Report* states that if present trends continue, the world in the year A.D. 2000 will be more crowded, more polluted, less stable ecologically, and more vulnerable to disruption than the world in which you and I are living today. Serious stresses involving population, resources, and environment are clearly visible for most of us. Despite greater material output, the world's people will be poorer in many ways than they are today. This is not a very rosy picture for those of us who claim to be God's stewards.

For hundreds of millions of the desperately poor, the outlook for food, clothing, shelter, and the other necessities of life will be no better. For many it will be far worse unless we act decisively as good stewards to change current trends.

POPULATION GROWTH

A storm cloud on the horizon in any discussion of the earth's future is the enormous growth in the world's population that will occur by 2000. According to the *Global 2000 Report's* projections, the world's population will increase 55 percent from 4.1 billion people in 1975 to 6.35 billion by 2000. All the problems we will discuss are already problems under the present levels of population. Such an increase in population means they can only get worse as we continue to break the stewardship agreement.

Most of the population growth (92 percent!) will occur in the world's less developed countries, areas that, in turn, often magnify the problem as they rapidly attempt to reach the scale of consumption they see as the model life-style established by the industrialized world, particularly Canada and the United States. We have to ask ourselves, therefore, "What kind of model are we depicting as God's stewards?"

In addition to rapid population growth, the less-developed countries will experience a dramatic movement of their rural population to cities and adjacent settlements, making them almost inconceivably overcrowded. For example, by the year 2000 Mexico City is projected to have more than 31 million people—roughly three times the present population of the entire New York metropolitan area. Calcutta will approach the 20 million mark, and Bombay, Cairo, Jakarta, and Seoul are expected to be in the 16 to 19 million range. Another four hundred cities around the world will have passed the million mark, many of them by several times!

As you can imagine, rapid urban growth between now and 2000 will put extreme pressures on sanitation, water and food supplies, shelter, health care, and job availability. It has been estimated that the less-developed countries will have to increase their urban services by two thirds by 2000 just to stay even with the 1975 levels, which are already almost indescribably poor compared to those enjoyed by most North Americans. In many large cities of the world—for example, Bombay, Calcutta, Mexico City, Rio de Janeiro, Seoul, and Taipei—at least a quarter of the population already lives in uncontrolled settlements, and the trend is toward sharp increases.

ECONOMIC GROWTH

Another major area of consideration is the distribution and use of the earth's limited resources. Repeatedly we have been reminded that there is a oneness of this planet and its people. But most of us are also aware that there is not a oneness in the distribution of the planet's resources to meet human needs. And because distribution is a primary factor in how well we are performing as stewards, we must consider the terrible inequalities in wealth and income among the earth's peoples.

There are several ways of making these comparisons. For example, North America has 6.2 percent of the world's population but 34.6 percent of the world's combined gross national product. On the other hand, Africa and Asia have 62.5 percent of the population but only 11.3 percent of the combined gross national product. Clearly, we use nearly six times our share of the combined gross national product, while Africa and Asia's share is only two tenths of what it should be.

These facts do not give most of us a very clear picture of the situation, primarily because gross national product somehow gets translated in our minds as "average income," and this completely ignores how the wealth is divided between the rich and the poor of any given country. In Kenya, for example, which currently has an average annual income of $170 per person, the richest 20 percent of the population receives nearly 70 percent of the income while the poorest 40 percent of the people receive only 10 percent. And this is apparently a fairly typical picture in most of the less-developed countries.

According to the *Global 2000 Report*, not only are the income differences between the wealthiest and poorest nations bad now, but they are projected to widen in the years ahead.

FOOD PRODUCTION AND DISTRIBUTION

The wide difference between poor and rich countries can also be seen when you look at the percentage of income used by the average person to buy food. Let us consider the pattern in eight countries:

United States	17%	Indonesia	50%
Great Britain	22%	Peru	52%
Japan	23%	Zaire	62%
USSR	38%	India	67%

It is easy to see that a great many of the world's people do not have much left over after they have bought food for themselves and their families. And when you compare the type of food consumption (and sometimes malnutrition) that goes on in our own land, where we spend such a small percentage of our income on food, to the malnutrition and hunger that exists in countries on the other end of the scale, you begin to realize the tremendous contrast that exists. Not only do we tend to eat too much, but we usually buy food that is overprocessed, not good for us in the long run, and wastefully packaged.

Going beyond this, to satisfy our demand for different kinds of food, many of us in North America look to other nations to produce and provide our food. For example, 99 percent of our coffee comes from foreign sources, as do 100 percent of our cocoa, 99 percent of our bananas, and 43 percent of our sugar. Food that is shipped to us cannot be eaten by the people who work hard to produce it. What does this say about our stewardship?

"But," you say, "they receive money for their coffee, and with those funds can buy other food." Wrong! Less-developed countries usually export unprocessed products, which sell at far lower prices than the processed or manufactured products they import from us. In the case of Tanzania, for example, more and more sisal (used to make rope) must be exported to afford the increasingly costly farm machinery needed for its production. Much of the land in the Dominican Republic is used to raise sugar cane for the United States and other wealthy countries. Some of the best farmland in northern Mexico is used to grow tomatoes so that people in the United States will have fresh tomatoes in the winter. And some of the best land in Haiti is used to produce cattle to make hamburgers for us!

According to the *Global 2000 Report*, the less-developed countries today produce 87 percent of their own food, but by the end of the century this figure could fall to 74 percent. One out of every eight people on earth is hungry most of the time. And in many countries up to 40 percent of the population is malnourished.

Hunger (or malnutrition) results when people consume fewer calories and less protein than their bodies need to live active, healthy lives. Malnutrition also increases susceptibility to disease, and about one out of every four children born in the less-developed countries dies before the age of five—mostly from nutrition-related causes.

HUNGER MYTHS

Misleading ideas about world hunger can only confuse our efforts to help, and there is significant controversy about the specific causes of world hunger. Experts are divided on the issue. Most of us have grown up with some false ideas (or myths) about why people are hungry.

Myth No. 1. There is hunger in the world because of a lack of food. False! There is enough food to feed everyone in the world adequately (with three thousand calories a day per person) if those who need it had the means to buy it, and if the available food were used reasonably. In Bangladesh, four million tons of rice accumulated after the 1974 floods because the large majority of the population was too poor to buy any.

Myth No. 2. There is hunger in the world because of the lack of land. False! Only 44 percent of the total cultivatable land is actually being cultivated. Many landowners consider their property an investment rather than a source of food, so they let large areas lie idle. Also, in many countries, the better part of the most fertile land is used to grow export crops. For example, production of coffee in Africa increased fourfold during the past twenty years, and the production of tea sixfold. The production of cocoa and cotton doubled, and sugar cane tripled. All of these crops were for export, to the detriment of the local population.

Myth No. 3. There is hunger because the earth is overpopulated. Well, the earth is overpopulated, but it is wrong to say this is why hunger exists. Statistics demonstrate that overpopulation is not a cause for famine. Hunger is not related to the number of people per acre, but to the agricultural system being used and the distribution system (whether those who cultivate the land can benefit from what is produced). China, for example, has only half the cultivatable land that India has, yet China has succeeded in eliminating obvious undernourishment.

Myth No. 4. The only solution to hunger is to produce more food. False! Right now politics favors modernization of agriculture in order to increase yields. But the new techniques only profit those who already own land, or have money or political influence. Farming methods have been "modernized"; ambitious irrigation plans have been carried out; "miracle" seeds, new pesticides, fertilizers, and machinery have become available. But who has come out better off? Farmers who already own land and have the ability to buy on credit—not the desperately poor and hungry. And the number of unemployed and landless is growing.

Myth No. 5. Only large property owners can solve the problem of hunger. False! Recent studies in Latin America, North America, and the U.S.S.R. have demonstrated that in reality smaller farmers are more efficient, particularly in providing food for the local population. When investments are concentrated on the large property owners, the landowners increase their holdings and tend to produce cash crops for export. Thus, their land is not producing food that could eliminate local hunger. For example, in Senegal, some development funds provided by relief organizations were used to irrigate the desert in order to cultivate eggplant and mango, which were then shipped to Europe.

Myth No. 6. It is necessary to increase the use of pesticides and fertilizers in spite of dangers to the environment. False! There are many substitutes for chemical pesticides and fertilizers, such as crop rotation, handpicking, and interplanting. The U.S. Environmental Protection Agency estimates that thirty years ago American farmers used 2,265 tons of insecticides and lost 7 percent of the crop before harvest. Now they use twelve times more, and the loss before harvest has almost doubled.

Myth No. 7. Hunger is pitting the rich countries against the poor countries. False! In reality, most of the average citizens of industrialized countries are united with the overwhelming majority of poor people around the world—whether we know it or not!—by the common menace of the growth of a few huge corporations that will soon control the global food system. Hunger will never be eliminated until we recognize the poor of the world as our neighbors and realize that our own consumption pattern is creating a suction force that diverts food from the very people who have grown it.

Myth No. 8. The world hunger problem can be solved by distributing food to the poor. Well, it is true that massive food distribution programs can help for a limited time. And Americans (among others) can begin to understand their interrelatedness with all people and adopt a simpler life-style in which they stop demanding imported food. But studies have shown that people will only cease to be poor and hungry when they control the means of providing and producing food for themselves. And the real questions for those of us who want to be good stewards are: How can control of the land get back into the hands of the people who need it? Who influences the distribution of food? And how can people be enabled to provide food for themselves?

LOSS OF AGRICULTURAL LAND

Perhaps the single most serious environmental development reported by the *Global 2000 Report* is the continued and accelerating deterioration and loss of agricultural land because of soil erosion, loss of nutrients, compaction of soils, increasing salinization, loss of cropland to urban development, and desertification resulting from shortage of water and vegetation cover.

Deterioration of soils is occurring rapidly in most of the less-developed countries, with the spead of desertlike conditions in drier regions and heavy erosion in wetter areas. Present annual global losses to desertification are estimated at about six million hectares. A hectare equals 10,000 square meters or 2.471 acres. According to these figures, the loss each year from desertification is equal to an area the size of Maine!

Desertification does not necessarily mean the creation of Saharalike sand deserts, but rather it includes a variety of ecological changes that destroy the vegetation and fertile soil, making the land useless for grazing or crops. The principal direct causes of desertification are overgrazing, destructive farming practices, and the overcutting of woody plants and trees to use for fuel.

Although soil loss and deterioration are especially serious in many of the less-developed countries, they are also affecting agricultural prospects in North America. For example, in 1975 the U.S. Department of Agriculture reported that soil loss on croplands amounted to three billion tons every year, or an average of nine tons per acre! And in places like California's San Joaquin and Imperial Valleys, which rely on extensive irrigation, millions of acres of productive land are threatened because of salinization (salt buildup in the soil).

In addition, the increased burning of dung and crop wastes for heating fuel has already deprived the land of nutrients and organic matter that could hold moisture and help prevent compaction. For the world's poor, these organic materials are often the only source of fertilizing nutrients needed to maintain the farmland's productivity. Those people who can least afford to buy chemical fertilizers are being forced to burn their only alternative! Most industrialized nations have increased their use of chemicals. So far this has compensated for the basic decline in soil condition. But heavy use of chemical fertilizers and pesticides also leads to losses of soil organic matter, reducing the capacity of the land to hold moisture. This leads to increased need for irrigation. Unfortunately, it is often very difficult to maintain the productivity of irrigated lands; the *Global 2000 Report* estimates that already about half of the world's irrigated land has been damaged to some degree by salinity, alkalinity, and waterlogging. Soil specialists have discovered that it is possible, but very slow and highly costly, to restore damaged land.

Loss of good farmland to urban encroachment is another problem affecting all nations of the world. Cities and factories are often located on the nation's best agricultural land—rich, well-watered, alluvial soils in gently sloping valleys. Cecil Andrus, former U.S. Secretary of the Interior, says that American farmland is being paved over for urban uses—highways, shopping centers, housing tracts, and airports—at a rate of three million acres a year. That is twelve square miles each day! And Mr. Andrus says in the last decade we have lost an area equal in size to Vermont, New Hampshire, Connecticut, New Jersey, and Delaware combined.

A Nigerian chieftain once said, "Land belongs to a vast family, of which many are dead, a few are living, and countless numbers are unborn." Today the quiet crisis of land loss and abuse haunts our planet, and the problem is much closer to home than most of us think.

THE ENERGY CRISIS—NO QUICK FIX!

The *Global 2000 Report's* energy projections show no early relief from the energy problems already being experienced by most of the world. And although the supply of petroleum-based energy is not expected to increase, because we are surely exhausting the supply, per capita energy consumption is estimated to be increasing everywhere. The largest increase in the next few years will be in the industrialized nations other than the United States. The percentage increase for the United States and most of the less-developed countries will be about the same—27 percent—but actual per capita energy consumption will be very different. By the year 2000 our per capita energy use is projected to be about 422 million BTU (British thermal units) annually, whereas in the less-developed countries it will be only 14 million BTU (up from 11 million in 1975).

Most of us in North America know that the cost of oil and other commercial energy sources is going up, but we are unaware that the supply of firewood in many parts of the world is going down at a terrific rate. The poor of the world use wood fires to heat their shelters and cook their food. Scarcities of wood are expanding. In the arid Sahel of Africa, for example, fuel wood gathering has become so hard that it is a full-time job requiring 360 person-days of work per household each year in some places! Areas around urban centers have become barren, and wood gatherers must travel fifty to one hundred kilometers each way to collect fuel wood. In some West African cities, urban families, too far from collectible wood, must spend 20 to 30 percent of their income on wood.

The shortage of fuel wood points to a decrease in energy for essential purposes. It also means that deforestation will be expanded, wood prices will go up, and greater amounts of dung and crop wastes will be used for cooking fires instead of being added to the soil as nutrients.

In North America, our energy concerns usually center on reasonable cost to both people and the environment. Some of our present supply problems come from overdependence on nonrenewable and increasingly expensive energy sources. Other problems stem from negative environmental and social impacts by the energy system. Still other problems are the result of our wasteful and unnecessary consumption.

Nuclear energy presents still further serious problems. The risk of radioactive contamination resulting from reactor accidents will increase, as will the potential for proliferation of nuclear weapons. No nation has yet conducted a demonstration program for the satisfactory disposal of radioactive waste, and the amount of waste is increasing rapidly. Several hundred thousand tons of highly radioactive spent nuclear fuel will be generated over the lifetimes of the nuclear plants proposed to be built before the end of this century. In addition to the radioactive waste created, nuclear power generation will produce millions of cubic meters of low-level radioactive wastes, and uranium mining and processing will lead to the production of hundreds of millions of tons of low-level radioactive tailings. It has not yet been shown that all of these high- and low-level wastes can be stored safely or otherwise disposed of without serious incidents. As good stewards we should note that some of these by-products have half-lives approximately five times as long as all of recorded history!

Although the projections of conventional industrial energy sources are gloomy because they are capital-intensive, large-scale, expensive, and often dangerous to the environment, there are some bright spots too. For example, the use of renewable energy sources has a broad potential for much of the world. As early as 1892 Chile had developed a solar still to produce clean water, and by 1912 Egypt had produced and installed a solar water pump for irrigation.

Considerable research and development in renewable energy sources is going on in Asia, Latin America, and Africa. Solar cells have been used successfully in Chile, Upper Volta, Niger, and India. Water power has been developed in Turkey and Afghanistan, and it has been reported that China has constructed at least fifty thousand small-scale plants to produce hydroelectricity. Argentina, Zambia, and Tanzania have carried out highly successful experiments with windmills. Brazil is producing ethanol from sugarcane and cassava. In the Philippines, coconut husks are being used as fuel in electric generating plants. And China is producing methane and fertilizer from animal dung.

WATER AND THE ATMOSPHERE

Among the emerging environmental stresses are some that affect the quality of the water we drink and the air we breathe.

The quality of the world's water has suffered because of our carelessness. Virtually all of the *Global 2000* projections point to increasing pollution of coastal ecosystems (estuaries, swamps, and salt marshes) that are used by 60 to 80 percent of commercially valuable marine fishery species for habitat at some point in their life cycles.

Pollution from heavy applications of pesticides has been widespread in North America, and though in the United States we have for the most part shifted away from the use of long-lived chemicals such as DDT, the persistent use of dangerous pesticides is projected for years to come, and is expected to quadruple between now and 2000.

Water pollution in the less-developed countries is likely to worsen as the urban population soars and industry expands. Already the water downstream from many cities is heavily polluted with sewage and wastes from mills, tanneries, refineries, and chemical plants.

Carbon dioxide buildup in the earth's atmosphere is another part of the total environmental dynamics that may be bringing about an end to human civilization as we know it. The result of the carbon dioxide buildup could be a significant alteration of precipitation patterns around the world and a rise of several degrees of temperature in the middle latitudes. Even a one-degree Celsius increase in average global temperature would make the earth's climate warmer than it has been anytime in the last thousand years! Scientists warn that a carbon dioxide–induced temperature rise is expected to be three or four times greater at the poles than in the middle latitudes. A five- to ten-degree increase in temperature at the poles could lead to the melting of the ice, in turn leading to a gradual rise in the sea level and forcing the abandonment of many coastal areas.

Acid rain is another major concern. Sulfur and nitrogen oxides from the burning of fossil fuels, especially coal, cause serious troubles because they combine with water vapors in the atmosphere to form acid rain. The effects of acid rain, seen in Norway, Sweden, Germany, Eastern Europe, Russia, Canada, and the United States, are not fully understood, but damage has already been observed in lakes, soils, forests, crops, nitrogen-fixing plants, and building materials.

In New York's Adirondack Mountains, 212 of the 2,200 lakes and ponds are acidic, dead, and fishless. Acid rain has killed aquatic life in at least 10 percent of New England's 226 largest freshwater lakes. And damage from acid rain has been reported in Minnesota, Wisconsin, Florida, and California.

But Canada suffers most severely. Environmental officials project the loss of 48,000 lakes by the end of this century if nothing is done to curb acid rain. Already, nearly 4,000 lakes in Ontario have become so acidified that they can no longer support trout and bass, and some 1,300 more lakes in Quebec are on the brink of destruction. In Nova Scotia, 9 rivers formerly used as spawning grounds by Atlantic salmon in the spring no longer teem with fish.

SPECIES EXTINCTION

The earth faces another urgent problem in the probable loss of plant and animal genetic resources. Parts of the *Global 2000 Report* suggest that 15 to 20 percent of all species now living on earth could be extinct by the year 2000. This would be brought about mainly by loss of wild habitat, but also in part because of pollution. Nearly two thirds of the extinctions projected will occur as a result of clearing of tropical forests. Some scientists point out the immense value of these genetic reservoirs. If they are preserved and carefully managed, tropical forests could be a sustainable source of new foods, pharmaceutical chemicals, natural predators of pests, building materials, fuel, and so on.

Current trends in the way we live and do things also threaten fresh- and saltwater fish. Physical alterations, such as damming, channelization, and drilling for oil in the seabed, and pollution by salts, acid rain, and other toxic chemicals are killing water life around the world.

Large mammals are being killed off too. Trophy hunters have been guilty for years in reducing herd numbers. International whaling quotas have been reduced, but in 1982 the number allowed to be killed was still 12,571 (of which only 206 were for Eskimos of Russia, Greenland, and the United States who need them for a food source). And grizzly bear populations have experienced almost a 40 percent drop from the early 1970's, falling victim to hunters and loss of habitat.

Some of the most important genetic losses will involve the extinction of varieties of cereal grains. Four fifths of the world's food supply is derived from less than two dozen plant and animal species. Wild strains are needed for breeding resistance to pests. But these variegated strains are rapidly diminishing as marginal wildlands are brought into cultivation.

NUCLEAR DESTRUCTION

In spite of all the other problems the world faces, both short- and long-term, the threat of total destruction from nuclear war is the chief problem seen by most Americans in the early 1980's. A Gallup poll conducted in 1981 is a vivid testimony to the growing awareness and concern of most North Americans about the likelihood of death and destruction caused by an exchange of nuclear weapons:

- 65% of American people are concerned about the possibility of a nuclear war.
- 68% believe there is some chance of an all-out nuclear war between the United States and the Soviet Union before 1992.
- 71% believe that a war between the United States and the Soviet Union would lead to a nuclear exchange.
- Only 9% believe they would have a good chance of surviving an all-out nuclear war.

Though warfare is as old as the history of humankind, attempts to control arms are relatively new. There were some successful efforts between world powers in the nineteenth century, and an agreement following World War One prohibited the use of poison gas. But proposals concerning nuclear weapons have taken a long time to negotiate and have been only minimally effective.

Twin revolutions in (1) the destructive power of nuclear weapons and (2) the speed, range, and accuracy of delivery systems have radically changed the picture of warfare that existed just a few decades ago during World War Two. Now whole countries can be completely destroyed in a matter of moments! A single missile can deliver a warhead more powerful than all the bombs dropped on Germany in World War Two and place it within a hundred meters of any target.

Although people do not agree on exactly why there is an arms race, we have been deeply engaged in one since 1946. Then there was just one weapon; there were more than 50,000 weapons in 1982. Trying to figure out who is leading the arms race is difficult because the various weapons are not equal. When all the variable factors are considered, it seems that the United States and the U.S.S.R. are roughly equal in strategic strength as this is written.

Whatever the case, both the United States and the Soviet Union have enough nuclear warheads to totally destroy the other country even if the other side attacks first without warning. This is referred to as mutually assured destruction (MAD). Estimates are that up to 120 million Russians would be killed in an all-out nuclear war and about 70 percent of their overall industrial capacity would be destroyed. Casualty figures would probably be slightly higher for the United States because we have a more urbanized society; up to 140 million Americans would die and more than 80 percent of our industry would be destroyed. In addition, an all-out nuclear war would certainly spread to Europe, and as many as 120 million Europeans would also die almost instantly.

By this time if you are wondering if your hometown would be targeted, you can assume that it probably would be. There are many more warheads than big cities, so it is likely that even some cities of 10,000 population would be attacked, especially if they have any industry, are a transportation center, or are near a military base of any kind.

A distinctive feature of nuclear war would be fallout—radioactive particles that would fall back to earth after the explosion. Fallout is a kind of poison that can be absorbed through the skin, breathed in, or eaten. It causes radiation sickness that often results in death. Because the radioactive particles are carried long distances by the winds, 75 percent of the rural area of the United States and all urban areas would be exposed to dangerous levels of fallout.

If you survived a nuclear war, you would find that the world as you know it today would be gone; the world that followed would be different, but no one can say exactly how. Most police officers, fire fighters, and government officials would be dead or seriously injured. Banks, courthouses, and official records would be gone. Paper money would be worthless. Food would be scarce—maybe even impossible to find, especially in urban areas. Water, gas, electric, and sewer systems would not operate for weeks at best, most likely for months, and possibly never again. Most of the things you care about would no longer exist, and every day for weeks after the war you could watch people you know and love die. You might even find yourself committing acts you would once have found deplorable in order to survive. There is a lot of truth in the statement of the Ground Zero organization, "The bad news is you might survive!"

Canada provides an excellent example of a developed nation that has not become a leader in the world's arms race. In a recent year, Canada spent $167 per person on its military budget, ranking it twenty-second in the world. During that same year, the United States spent $465 per person and ranked seventh in per capita spending for the military. With its relatively low arms budget, Canada spent $676 per person on education, ranking it third in the world. The United States spent $557, ranking it eighth. Canada's per capita spending on health was $460, ranking sixth, whereas the United States spent $304, ranking twelfth. So although Canada is deliberately behind in the arms race, it appears to be well ahead of some others in the race toward the well-being of its citizens.

A WORD TO STEWARDS

It is easy to see that the original agreement is still being broken. The era of cheap and abundant energy is over for all of us—and for much of the world's population it never even started! The sources of energy currently supporting industrial-technological society are being depleted rapidly and are not renewable. The present worldwide patterns of organizing and distributing food are lacking in justice, sustainability, and the participation of people. And the threat of nuclear war hangs over us all!

However, in the midst of this terrible situation, God continues to call us to positions of responsibility to the rest of creation and to the poor and helpless among us. And the promise is that the new era that must come offers fresh possibilities for humane communities and a restored creation.

6.
The Task for Us Now

David asked the age-old question of our place in the universe when in the Eighth Psalm he questioned, "What is man, that you think of him; mere man, that you care for him?" For most of human history this was a very natural question to ask as our ancestors worked to survive in intimate daily contact with, and total dependence on, the natural world. It is worth noting that the Bible never even hints at a separation between the physical and the spiritual, nor does the Bible have a word for what we today call "the world of nature." There is not even a word in Hebrew for "nature."

The Scriptural witness is abundant: *Ps. 24:1* tells us, "The world and all that is in it belong to the Lord; the earth and all who live on it are his." Again, *Ps. 19:1* reminds us: "How clearly the sky reveals God's glory! How plainly it shows what he has done!" Throughout the Old Testament there are hymns that sing of God's glory in the creation and recall God's relationship to all of creation. One of the most touching is *Ps. 104.*

A fact that startles most of us today is that the Bible rarely speaks of our domination over any or all other aspects of creation. I have already pointed out one of the only two references that can be found, *Gen. 1:28.* The other reference is *Ps. 8:5-6* in which David, marveling at God's care for humanity, remarked, "Yet you made him inferior only to yourself, you crowned him with glory and honor. You appointed him ruler over everything you made; you placed him over all creation."

These have been the "proof texts" of the industrial age's general attitude that nature is nothing more than the warehouse that holds the raw materials for the transformation of society in history.

American Christians who reflect theologically on issues of global hunger, the environment, justice, and the definite possibility of nuclear destruction will find a common bond with the poor in Third World countries. The experience of powerlessness and the struggle for liberation are concerns that connect us all to the

Biblical understanding of God's love for creation and God's actions for salvation and liberation.

But as we consider the task for us now as stewards, we soon find that we must act on the basis of an environmental justice ethic; that is, our behavior must be consistent with our beliefs, our actions suited to our faith commitments about the environment, God, and our neighbors. These concerns encompass more than dollars, food production, or political philosophy. Instead, our relationship to justice and the environment is a very real moral issue!

THEOLOGICAL ROOT CAUSES

In examining some aspects of the Judeo-Christian heritage and religion, we must look at a number of theological root causes in addition to the social, political, and economic factors involved. A brief study of these theological root causes may help us understand our involvement, or lack of involvement, in the search for solutions to the scandals the world faces today. The theological root causes I am listing are intended for debate, not uncritical acceptance.

Neglect of the Scriptures

Certain Bible passages have been emphasized while others, dealing with social justice, have been neglected. For example, how many of us remember that ill-treatment of the poor was a major sin which led to the judgment and later destruction of Sodom (*Ezek. 16:49*)? Or why do we encourage children to memorize *Isa. 1:18*, "You are stained red with sin, but I will wash you as clean as snow," but not to memorize (and put into practice) *Isa. 1:17*, "See that justice is done—help those who are oppressed, give orphans their rights, and defend widows"?

So often our interpretation of the Scriptures is influenced by our economic status. Down through the years, and even today, comfortable Christians have preferred to spiritualize the promises and warnings about wealth and poverty. Because of the Reformers' experiences in the church of their day, justification has far more priority than justice in our current theology. And although justice for the poor is high on the list of concerns in both the Old and New Testaments, most of our creedal statements do not deal directly with poverty issues.

The Two-Kingdom Theory

Some theologians like to speak of God ruling the universe in two realms or kingdoms. One kingdom is the realm of the believing community, the church, where the primary principle is God's grace. In the other kingdom, the realm of human order (including the institutions of family, industry, and government), the primary principle is law. This theory is often twisted and misunderstood among Christians. We have tried to limit Almighty God to the first kingdom—the realm of eternal salvation—and exclude God from the realm of everyday life. The United States policy of separation of church and state has been thought of at times as a doctrine that excludes God's will and activity from politics. We ought to ask ourselves if a misuse of the two-kingdom theory ever leads us away from taking strong stands on public issues, either as individual believers or as the corporate church? Does such a misinterpretation support a silent majority acceptance of the social and political status quo?

Silence of the Prophetic

The old-time Biblical prophets were active advocates for social justice. They exposed the social inequalities of their day and called the people back to their covenant relationship with God.

In many subtle ways the prophetic call is being muted, if not altogether silenced, in our churches today. The desire for security, coupled with the pressure to meet the church budget and increase membership while avoiding conflict, often discourages the application of the Scriptures to current social and political issues. For many of us, the close tie we have with the benefits of economic prosperity makes it very difficult to speak prophetically.

The Call for Radical Discipleship

Some liberation theologians remind us that Christology (the life and teachings of Jesus Christ) is at the center of our problem regarding social justice and the environmental crisis. They point out that many Christians have ignored the fundamental principles and values preached and acted on by Jesus. They remind us that frequently nowadays Christ is reduced to a sort of sublime abstraction, and that the call to follow the historical Christ of the New Testament is lost. Therefore, many church members remain neutral or indifferent toward the flagrant inequalities in our society and around the world. To put it very simply, the call to repentance has not carried with it the call to change our accumulation of wealth while others go hungry. The radical imperative to love our neighbor, to seek justice, and to be peacemakers is set aside because of our greater concern to avoid conflicts or to not adversely affect our own pension fund.

Solidarity with the Poor

The God of Biblical faith is basically identified with those who had been dispossessed. The Old Testament prophets constantly were speaking out in behalf of the poor, the weak, and the powerless. In the fullness of time Jesus came to preach good news to the poor, and Luke quoted Jesus when he said, "Happy are you poor; the Kingdom of God is yours!" (*Luke 6:20*).

Down through the years, many parts of the Christian church have failed to understand completely the nature of poverty or the problems of the poor and dispossessed. Nearly always church members have tended to identify more with the middle and upper classes. But some modern-day prophets are saying that the church of the future may no longer be divided between Catholic and Protestant, or liberal and conservative, but between the church of the poor and dispossessed and the church of the rich and powerful.

Individualism

The Christian faith is a very personal matter for most of us in North America. It involves a very personal relationship with Jesus, whom we confess as Lord and

Savior. But it was never intended to be a private matter! Any spirituality removed from the social and political realities of the day is not Biblical. An ancient Hebrew puts it this way: "Any religion that is taught apart from life leads to a life apart from religion."

Here in North America, the rugged individualism of our frontier days has crept into our theology and blurred our sense of community and responsibility. During the past years, too much of our preaching and teaching has tended to develop a personal conscience but not a social conscience, and so most of us are careful to lead honest, clean, moral lives, but not to be overly concerned for our brothers and sisters around the world. Too much emphasis on individualism can also encourage a competitive spirit that makes cooperation between people, congregations, and denominations less likely. Personal goals then become more important than the good of the entire community.

Civil Religion

Patriotism is sometimes too closely tied with Christianity in North America. What results is a sort of civil religion, which approves the culture and society without first judging their qualities. And there is a very strong temptation on the part of many church and political leaders to identify the American cause with the cause of Almighty God. It is not surprising, therefore, that some of our people confuse the two causes and become very defensive toward criticism of our government and economic system.

Triumphalism

The Christian faith has always held a strong belief in the return of Jesus Christ and his ultimate victory over sin and death. An overemphasis on this, called "the theology of glory" by some, can make Christians neglect to take any responsibility for bringing about necessary changes in global society today. As someone once said, "We can become so heavenly minded that we are no earthly good!" In many areas of the world our only consolation to the poor has been a reminder that they will be rewarded in heaven if they believe in Jesus and patiently endure their poverty and hunger and illness while we continue to accumulate great wealth. How easily we forget (or ignore) Jesus' example of the rich man and Lazarus (*Luke 16:19-31*).

BENEDICT AND FRANCIS

Two figures from the Christian church have set precedents for Western environmental views. They are being closely reexamined today, when so many Christians around the world are struggling to understand the environmental crisis we face and evolve a new "theology of the earth" to help us plot a course of action. These two men, Benedict of Nursia (480–543) and Francis of Assisi (1182–1226), developed theologies of the earth that have been called Benedictine stewardship and Franciscan conservatism.

Amidst the warring factions of the turbulent sixth century, Benedict founded one of the greatest monasteries of Christendom at Monte Cassino in Italy. The son of a Roman noble, Benedict was only nineteen or twenty years old when he retreated to a cave in the desert of Subiaco, forty miles east of Rome, where he lived for slightly more than three years as a hermit. Fame began to come, and the monks of a neighboring monastery urged him to become their leader. Benedict proved too strict for them and returned to his hermit cave where he founded the famed Abbey of Monte Cassino, which eventually became the center from which his rule spread.

In about 529, Benedict drew up his rule for his monks with the intention of banishing idleness. This was a sort of combination of Latin civil law and Greek humanism harnessed to the service of the Christian gospel.

The basic tenet of Benedict's rule is that to labor is to pray. Benedict combined that which is intellectual with that which is physical, nurturing both practical and theoretical skills in the same person. Benedict's rule stresses not absolute dominion over nature, but stewardship and wise management of nature, resulting in a maintenance of environmental quality. Thus, the physical work of most of the Benedictine monks was directed toward the environment in what we might well call creative intervention, where human activity is developed favoring a creative and harmonious relationship between people and the environment.

It is worth noting that entire chapters of the Benedictine rule discuss the care of the sick and needy outside of the monastery, and the distribution of food and clothing to the poor.

When Francis was born in twelfth-century Italy, he entered a world of social upheaval. Before his time, most of Europe included two rigid classes of people—nobility and common folk. The nobility offered protection, and the common people served the nobility as farm workers, merchants, and craftsmen. However, the opening of new markets during the Crusades brought wealth and greater power to the merchants. Soon the merchants broke out of the feudal system and took control of towns like Assisi. Francis was born into a home of this "new rich" merchant class that loved war-making, moneymaking, and wearing elaborate clothing to display its wealth.

The poor people in the towns controlled by the merchants were worse off by far than they had been under the feudal system. Instead of being protected, the poor were used by greedy and cruel merchants for slave-type labor or for fighting the brutal wars that were waged between towns. The many common people who had no employment were forced to beg for survival.

The church at this time was at the peak of its worldly political power and was very corrupt. The pope and many bishops depended on armies to enforce their rule at home while "Christian armies" slaughtered the "infidels" in the Middle East.

Francis stands, in his humble and peaceful way, as one of the radicals of the Christian faith. However, a study of his life calls into question two stereotypes: Francis of Assisi as quiet and serene (like his statue), and as primarily a nature lover. The truth is that Francis was a passionate, extravagant, assertive, charming preacher and singer whose primary concern was to follow Jesus on the way to the cross. He centered his life in Christ, the Christ who emptied himself (*Phil. 2:5-11*) and became poor. Francis understood this poverty to be Jesus' total dependence on God. In life, Jesus depended on God by owning nothing, and thus trusted God completely for daily bread. In death, Jesus gave up everything—his robe, his ministry, his disciples, his family, his dignity, his life—and trusted totally in God.

This "emptying" was the pattern for the life of Francis. He became poor by giving away everything and living the risky life of trusting God for daily bread. Near the end of his life he gave up the one thing he still possessed, the brotherhood of monks that he led. The brotherhood had left Francis' vision of total poverty for a more "realistic" way of life. In his forsakenness, Francis felt the pain of Christ's crucifixion.

When Francis became poor (in the sense of being dependent on God for daily sustenance), he saw himself at one with everyone and everything in creation that also depends on God. In joyful dependency he was connected to everything. Thus he spoke of brother deer, sister bird, brother wolf, brother sun, sister moon, and mother earth. In absolute identification with nature, he recognized the universality of all creatures and the sanctity of each organism in its own right (regardless of its utility to humans) as the handiwork of God. Nor did he neglect the same respect for plants or inanimate brethren such as water, wind, and fire. In the totality of his environment Francis served his Lord!

Sadly, in the American experience, the stewardship of Benedict over nature has been mutated into conflict with nature. And the loving, joyful conservatism of Francis toward our natural world has been withheld from our brother and sister human beings. And so we ask, as our abused, overburdened earth groans, and as people cry out for answers, what model might exist for the future care of the earth and its inhabitants.

A NEW ENVIRONMENTAL ETHIC

The ideals and teachings of both Francis and Benedict can be synthesized into a new environmental ethic that can lead to action on our part, particularly as we help others learn how we can all fulfill our responsibility as stewards of creation.

The Franciscan philosophy of equality fits in well with the relatively new science of ecology. In recognizing the intimate relationship between an object and its environment, ecology is the one science that has the ability to recapture the personality of nature. A number of modern speakers have equated the rights and needs of people with the rights and needs of the earth, and thus a concern for the sanctity of an individual quite naturally results in a concern for the global environment.

The disparity between our environmental ethic and our actual deeds could be bridged by following the example set before us by Benedict, establishing a society that in word and deed respects the rights of the earth and all its inhabitants. Such a society would balance technological innovation with ecological intelligence. I believe a society that does not idolize productivity alone but respects the dignity of the individual in work and is based on the voluntary simplicity of providing only sufficient quantities of food, clothing, and shelter could deal with the environment as if it had rights and not feel the need to threaten its neighbors with nuclear destruction.

The guilt of our ecological crisis has been chiefly laid on the citizens of North America, particularly those of us who come out of the Judeo-Christian tradition. And many of us have pounded our breasts while crying out, "*Mea culpa, mea maxima culpa!*—My fault!" Yet at the same time we enjoy the freedom to think, inquire, criticize, and change.

An environmental ethic is a philosophical view involved with morality and character, said the late Sigurd F. Olson in his last book, *Of Time and Place*. One of North America's best-known ecologists and interpretive naturalists, Olson argued that persons are not born with a feeling for ethics and the land, nor can children always simply comprehend its meanings through what they see in nature. Youths seldom have it, but as they mature into adults they begin to grasp a vague sense of oneness and belonging. In old age they gain perspective and wisdom, and can look back into the past and forward into the future. With our intergenerational programmatic concerns, we will involve participants of all age groups who can share their ideas, questions, and faith with us as colearners, coplanners, and resource people while sensing the interdependent relationships that exist in all creation.

My prayer is that we can take time to reevaluate the relationship between God, nature, and ourselves and that we will unite with one another in reaffirming our commitment as God's stewards of creation. It is vital for us to realize that as stewards of God's creation we are called not only to care for the earth in a just and sustaining way but also to share what we have with others even to the point of being needy ourselves. (See *Luke 6:30* and *ch. 21:1-4.*)

Here are five points you can ponder with your campers as you consider your role in environmental stewardship:

1. Everything belongs to God; we merely use it while we are here. God has given us control over the earth but did not intend for us to misuse air, soil, or water. God gave us control, but also gave us the responsibility to take care of the gift.

2. We should use no more than our share. Earth provides enough to satisfy every person's needs, but not every person's greeds!

3. We should try to see that everyone gets a fair share.

4. We should keep things in balance, pulling back as well as taking.

5. We should leave the world in good shape for those who will come after us.

PART THREE:
Learning Activities

7.
The Gift of Land and Water

Messengers of environmental gloom and doom seem to run with abandon today. The fact that in our camps we are seriously considering how we can be better stewards of creation indicates that we have chosen not to join that footrace. Rather we are taking time to give thought to our fragile ecological balance—to ponder what we might do to maintain our environmental quality and to improve it.

BIBLICAL INSIGHTS

The Bible does provide a guide to our relationship with creation, and as we work with our campers we should prayerfully reflect on the following five points which, I believe, will assist us as we face the environmental peril:

1. At no place does the Bible speak of a radical separation between the physical and the spiritual. The Biblical writers never thought of nature as a separate realm without relationships to God or to humanity. Christians do not believe in "a world of nature" that is detached from us or that exists independently from God.

2. At no point does the Bible give us any kind of permission to dominate nature that would at all justify the reckless, wasteful, and selfish exploitation of the environment we have witnessed. The idea of dominion, which is so often twisted, really means exercising dominion only as Almighty God does—the Creator God who sustains, upholds, and is glorified by all creation.

3. In the history of Israel, recorded in the Old Testament, we can see a model for us to follow. The central part of that history deals with the land as a promised gift from God to manage. The danger then, as now, was the desire to own it, possess it, and rule it. The gift of land is always conditional, dependent on living with the land as if both of us belong to God.

4. The New Testament clearly teaches that the work of Christ's redemption extends to all of creation. Through Christ's death and resurrection not only are we reconciled to God the Father but our broken relationship with creation is restored. This was certainly Paul's stirring message in *Rom. 8:19-23*.

5. The resurrection of Christ's body brings with it the strong promise that all of creation is renewed, transformed, and made into a new creation through God's grace. As we take steps to renew our commitment as God's stewards of creation, we would do well to realize what God has already done for us through the power of the resurrection!

JOINT LEARNING EXPERIENCES

Environmental life-style education almost always demands a "hands-on" experience. It is fundamental knowledge that the individual camper, of whatever age, will learn best from direct, purposeful experiences.

In the next several pages we are going to suggest a number of activities you and your campers can participate in as joint learning experiences. Some will also help improve the care of the campsite.

Where Does Soil Come From? Divide your group into several groups of two to four campers. Ask each group to collect some dirt from a different area, filling a tall glass jar about one-fourth full. Then add water until the jar is about two-thirds full.

Ask the campers to shake each jar vigorously for three or four minutes and then put the jar down on a level spot and let the dirt and water mixture settle for about half an hour. After half an hour ask the campers to draw a diagram showing the various layers in the jar. Campers can identify and label each layer.

They will see that soil particles differ considerably; some are harder than others and some do not break apart as easily as others. Rock pebbles and sand will probably settle to the bottom of the jar first. Settling more slowly will be smaller pieces, usually identified as silt. Clay particles will probably stay suspended the longest, making the water murky.

Most soils are made up of a mixture of sand, silt, and clay in various combinations. The size of the different particles is important. It has a lot to do with how well water will pass through the soil and how well the soil will hold water for plant roots.

Be sure to discuss the results of your investigation with the campers. Take time to look around the camp for examples of layering (on exposed road cuts, stream beds, or mountain sides). Check the site for signs of erosion, and talk about ways the erosion could be prevented. Be certain to look at the soil in the camp garden and talk about how it could be improved, and why.

Soil Compaction. Select several areas where there has been a lot of foot traffic (like on a main trail or in front of the camp canteen), and several other areas where it appears no one usually walks. Mark off study plots measuring, say, 2 meters by 2 meters.

Divide your group of campers up so that there is one smaller group for each study area. Ask the campers to count and classify the natural cover and litter (living and dead plants, leaves, insects) on their study area. Then ask the campers to measure the soil's compaction by checking the average depth to which a knife or icepick penetrates the soil when dropped four or five times from a height of 1.5 meters (for safety, a staff member should be enlisted to drop the knife or icepick).

Next have the campers measure the infiltration rate of water in their study area. They can do this by securing a No. 10 can from the camp kitchen, cutting out both ends, and placing the can in a hole in the soil. Fill the can with water, and check the time it takes for all the water to infiltrate into the soil.

Compare the information obtained at the various study areas, and discuss with your campers. Some sample questions to discuss are the following:

How does soil compaction influence water infiltration and runoff?

How does soil compaction affect the types and amounts of vegetation?

In what ways could any of this be improved?

In what areas of the camp could similar improvements be made? How? Could the campers help with a project?

Erosion Study. Ask your campers to select two equally sloping study areas on the campsite. One area should be covered with bare soil only. A road cut would do well. The second study area should have good vegetation cover—for example, grass, small plants, or moss.

Pour equal amounts of water over the two slopes and observe the results. Then discuss what you have seen. Here are several sample questions to discuss:

How did the vegetation affect the rate at which the water moved downhill?

On which slope did the water reach farthest downhill, and why?

What happened to any debris on the bare slope?

How could the erosion be prevented?

What possible steps could be taken at other locations on the campsite to prevent possible erosion in the future: along roads and trails? in the garden, near buildings, or by the lake or stream?

Give examples of other causes of erosion, and possible ways in which the erosion could be prevented.

Sandbag Construction. The use of sandbags is a simple but effective way to prevent or reduce floodwater damage and erosion. Properly filled and placed, sandbags can act as a barrier to divert moving water.

Sandbags can be used successfully to prevent water from leaving leveed streams and to direct current flow away from possible landslide areas, as well as to protect buildings.

Recycling. Many camps have already started at least some limited recycling program, and you can encourage your campers to join in the effort. Recycling is good for the environment. For example, paper that is recycled reduces the demand for pulp from forests, which in turn results in fewer trees being cut down. At the same time, using recycled paper to produce "new" paper requires only about half as much energy as making the same paper from scratch. It also requires fewer manufacturing steps, wastes less water, and uses less chemicals. In some areas, paper mills are buying recyclable paper as well as glass products and cans. Individuals and groups can profit at the same time they are helping the environment! Now we are going to talk about several special ways to recycle different things.

Art from Junk. In this activity you will be helping your campers learn that wornout, discarded materials may be reused in another form. They can also increase their recognition of artistic composition and gain some insight into creating objects of beauty.

Start with a "junk hike" around or near the campsite. Have the campers collect all the junk and litter they find (without considering what it was or how it might be used). Roadsides and vacant lots can be especially fruitful in this quest, and old community dumps can be a positively delightful place to spend an afternoon searching. When you have returned to your craft center, have each camper fashion some "art" objects from his or her found objects, or perhaps simply arrange them in an exhibit.

Composting. Another way to recycle is by composting. This is usually associated with gardening, and your camp may already be composting its kitchen waste as well as leaves and weeds from the garden and animal droppings. This is a good project in which to involve your campers because it is another activity that most of them can continue at home.

A compost pile is simply any collected pile of vegetation, manure, and other organic material that is allowed to decay, usually for the purpose of fertilizing a garden and conditioning the soil. In its simplest form it is just a heap of garden cuttings and kitchen scraps. Most people, however, prefer to enclose it in a bin or some other container. Composting is not a quick project because it generally takes a while to build a bin, quite a while to collect the materials you want to compost, and several months at least for the collected materials to "ripen."

Before you teach your campers some specific methods of composting, · they should understand several principles governing nearly all composting.

1. The smaller the particle size of your compost material, the faster the decomposition, because bacteria can attack more surface area faster. So, if possible, shred up your garden cuttings and kitchen scraps.

2. The bacteria in the pile need nitrogen or the decomposition will go slowly. Usually you can be sure there is enough nitrogen by adding fresh manure or blood meal here and there throughout the pile.

3. For the bacterial action to occur, the compost pile must heat up. The degree of heat depends primarily on the size of the pile. A small pile will lose heat and the bacterial action will slow down. But too high a pile is bad also, because the weight will compress the lower materials, shutting off the air supply to the bacteria.

4. Moisture is also necessary for decomposition to take place. Most compost experts agree that 40 to 60 percent moisture is about right. This is about as wet as a squeezed-out wet sponge. You can test for moisture by putting your hand in the pile and feeling it. Watch out, however, because it will probably be pretty hot— 130 to 160 degrees Fahrenheit! if it does not feel moist enough, just add some water until it feels right.

5. Most compost piles need turning, so that the outside materials become the center where most of the action takes place. This also allows for air to penetrate the pile. You can turn the material with a shovel or a pitchfork.

6. When the pile is "ripe," the materials will have been converted into a crumbly brown substance with the smell of good earth. The material will have decreased in volume as the decomposition took place; most piles reduce down to about half their original size.

Garbage-Can Compost. Find an old, galvinized twenty- or thirty-gallon garbage can (most camps usually have plenty that are not much good anymore). Punch several holes in the bottom. Put the can up on a few bricks or flat rocks. Be careful to put the can someplace where moisture from the decaying garbage will not run out and hurt anything. Inside the can put a three-inch layer of soil or some peat moss. Some people like to add some fishing worms to the soil at the bottom. Add a three-inch layer of kitchen garbage, then a two-inch layer of garden cuttings, and so on until the can is full. Keep the lid on the can except when you are filling it. By the way, you do not need to worry about the moisture content of this kind of bin nor does it need to be turned. The ripe compost will be ready in three or four months, so the compost you make this summer will be ready for the camp's garden next spring.

Composting in a Bin. There is no doubt that it is easier and neater to compost in a bin than in a heap, which starts to spread out as it grows and as you turn it. You can make a square bin out of wood. One of the best ideas I ever saw was a bin that was made of 1" x 12" rough planks to form a bin about 3 feet high and 2½ feet square. Four boards, 1 inch thick and 30 inches long, were nailed together to form a bottomless box. Build three bottomless boxes like this. Then set one box on the ground and stack the other two on top of it to make a bin. The cleverest idea was to put three 1½-inch PVC pipes with holes drilled in them every inch or so between each layer of boxes. These allow air to get right into the center of the bin so it is not necessary tor turn the compost.

When the compost is decomposing and has sunk below the level of the top box, take that box off the bin, and place it in the ground as the first level in a new bin. As the compost in the original bin reduces even more, take the second box off and place it on the new bin.

Composting in a Plastic Bag. You can produce an entirely acceptable compost in a large, dark-colored plastic bag, the kind used to line garbage cans. Be sure to conduct this composting operation in a remote part of the garden because although it is effective, it really smells to high heaven!

Inside the bag put a two-inch layer of soil or peat moss. Randomly add almost any kind of kitchen garbage—vegetable and fruit scraps, coffee grounds, egg shells, and so forth. You can add some yard cuttings, but mostly you want gooey, moist garbage. Keep the bag tightly closed between fillings. When the bag is full, put it out in full sunlight for about three weeks. the compost will "cook" and be ready for use.

Unlike the other methods of composting, this one uses a kind of bacteria that do not need air, nor does the compost need turning.

The complete compost can be added to your garden as a soil conditioner and as nutrients for your plants and vegetables, which they can use immediately because you have allowed the bacterial decomposition to take place in the compost bin. Gardens that lack composted organic materials usually are not so productive as those that have had compost added.

Controlling Pests and Diseases in the Garden. Many gardeners "go bugs" over insects in their garden. Unhappily, most of them rely on chemical sprays to get rid of the pests. Warfare in the garden may be justified, but the use of many chemicals is a form of insect-insanity.

There are a number of ways to get rid of garden pests, and most of these you can put into practice with your campers in the camp garden. The first thing to remember to tell your campers is that many factors determine whether insects are going to attack your plants. Weather is one of the major deciding factors. Most insects are influenced by the temperature and length of the day (as are your vegetables). Chemicals are apt to get rid of the pests but will also destroy the balance of nature, so I suggest several simple, safe, and easy methods you can teach your campers to keep your garden vigorous and healthy.

Keep the Garden Clean! The first step in getting rid of pests is to keep the garden clean. Get rid of all dead weeds and clean up piles of leaves and trash; move any piles of boards away from the garden area; and do not leave fallen fruit, vegetables, or leaves around. Some of the organic material can be put in your compost bin (but burn all diseased plants, do not compost them). Do not create hiding places or breeding grounds for insects or disease. Keep the garden clean!

Get Physical with the Pests. In some cases the easiest method of getting rid of pests is simply to use your fingers to pick them off the plants. This will not work with most flying pests, however. Maybe with your campers you can have a contest to see who can gather the most pests. Slugs or snails can be crushed between two boards or dropped in an old coffee can with some salt in the bottom. My experience is that a couple of ducks in a garden will keep the snail population down, but the ducks also enjoy some of the tender, young plants.

The Old Soap and Water Treatment. Another very effective way to clean up on the pests is by mixing twenty tablespoons of soap flakes with six gallons of water.

Then spray the plants, especially when you are bothered by scale insects like aphids.

Using "Fire to Fight Fire." In most nurseries you can buy sacks of ladybugs which you can turn loose in your garden. The ladybugs will go around gobbling up many pests, like aphids, thrips, tree lice, and the eggs and larvae of many other insects that will destroy your garden if they get the chance.

Protection from Animals. In addition to insects and disease, some animals will also be a nuisance in your camp garden. Gophers will attack from below and drag your vegetables away down their tunnels or nibble on the roots until the plant is dead (before you even know the gopher is around). Some gardeners insist that the best protection against gophers is a small sort of windmill that sets up a vibration in the ground that gophers are said not to tolerate.

Rabbits, raccoons, and deer appreciate good gardens too, and will be uninvited guests as often as possible. The best protection is a good fence.

Birds are a mixed blessing. They will feed on insects that are eating your garden. But they may also go after seedlings, fruit on trees, and berries. I have found the best protection is a plastic netting available at garden centers. You can drape it over plants and small trees. Another idea would be to have a scarecrow-building contest among the campers. You could see who built the scariest, the most original, the funniest, and so forth. Be sure to remember to take photographs to be used in publicity for next year!

The Water Crisis. The *Global 2000 Report* indicates that water shortages and the deterioration of water quality, already serious in many parts of the world, will probably become far worse by the end of this century. Population growth alone will at least double the demand for water in nearly half the countries of the world. Still greater increases will be needed to improve the standards of living.

Millions of children die every year in the world because they drink polluted water. Nearly 20,000 babies in India do not live to celebrate their first birthday because they are brought up on unsafe water. In order for your campers to understand the global water crisis, we must help them step into another world, at least in their imaginations. To do this you might have them lie down quietly, relaxed, with eyes closed. Then you can lead them on a "fantasy journey." It is best to describe briefly that you will be reading some descriptions and they should try to picture the scene in their mind's eye without talking, laughing, or making any other sounds. Here is a sample script. Read it slowly and softly:

> Now that you are relaxed, picture yourself as someone your own age living in a faraway land, a land that is very different from this country. You and your family live in a small hut at the edge of the village. No one in the village has running water. So you have no flush toilet and no sink or faucets. Like your neighbors, you and your brothers and sisters, your mother and father, and your old grandmother who lives with you "go to the bathroom" out in a field near your hut, usually before sunrise or after sunset. You don't have many clothes, but your mother and older sisters try to keep those you have clean by washing them in the nearby lake. That is where you bathe and wash your hands, also. That is the same lake where your family gets its drinking and cooking water. You and your whole family usually have diarrhea or other diseases you get from contaminated water. Often you are too sick to work. There is no doctor or nurse or drugstore in your village. No one in your village has even a basic education about health or sanitation. Your little baby sister is very ill with a high fever and will probably die tonight. You are usually hungry, but there is no food.

Ask the campers if they can describe how they felt (not what the scene in their head looked like). Discuss the global water crisis with them. Be aware that alerting them to the crisis, particularly if they think the crisis is far from them, may overwhelm them. Help them to understand at least part of the magnitude and complexity of the water sanitation problems, including those in North America and in your particular area. Help them to understand, also, that solutions are possible!

The United Nations has declared 1981–1990 as "The International Drinking Water Supply and Sanitation Decade." This is a worldwide problem, and there are probably serious water or sanitation problems near your camp and undoubtedly near some of your campers' homes. A 1971 U.S. Public Health Survey of 969 public water systems showed that 41 percent delivered water of inferior quality; 36 percent of the water contained dangerous bacteria or chemicals exceeding safe limits; 9 percent of the systems were potentially dangerous; 79 percent were not inspected by health officials even once a year; and 77 percent of the water plant operators were poorly trained.

Besides the problems of poor water quality and the concern for adequate supplies, there is another crisis about which we hear very little—distribution systems that are getting old and falling apart. Beneath our feet water pipes and sewer pipes crisscross one another, and many have deteriorated to such a point that the contents of one can contaminate the other.

With your campers, inspect as much of the camp's water system as you can. Where does the water come from? Is it treated? How? By whom? Is it checked by a health official? How? How often? Where is the last report and what does it say? Make the same kind of inspection of the camp's sewage system. What kinds of improvements can be made to either system? How could the camp save on the amount of water it uses? What other effects would this have, and on whom?

What are the central water concerns in your state? in your community? In what ways are these concerns being responsibly addressed? What steps can you and your campers take (as individuals or as a group) to preserve or restore water quality?

What are some of the signs of a water crisis in America? in the world? What can we do to help solve water problems in other parts of the world? What can *we* do to save water?

Using Biodegradable Products. Some chemicals used around the camp, especially detergents and insecticides, may not break down after they are used but will persist indefinitely. They show up in rivers and drinking water supplies, accumulate in the soil and in the food we eat, and upset the balance of nature. We will discuss this problem further when we talk about "Justice for Wildlife" in Chapter 11.

With your campers, check the camp kitchen and see if the detergent is biodegradable. Will it break down and rejoin nature, or will it be a threat to life? Check the kind of insecticides the camp uses. Find out what chemicals are banned, or at least controlled, in your state or province. While you are checking biodegradables, check to see now much of the camp's solid waste is not biodegradable. How can this be improved? Can you help? Will you?

Forest Resources. A forest is a plant and animal community that is dominated by trees. Many of our camps are located in forests, and we have an opportunity to study them firsthand.

Unfortunately, the forests of the world have been disappearing for many years.

The *Global 2000 Report* indicates that if the present trend continues, forests in the less-developed nations of the world will decline 40 percent by the end of the century.

Only in recent years have most Americans started to realize that forests, as well as clean water, pure air, and the land itself, are not only valuable but also vulnerable. Today, there is a growing recognition that the relationship between human beings and the natural environment is one of mutual dependency—if natural resources are despoiled, our living conditions deteriorate and people suffer.

At the time European people arrived, over 40 percent of the land in the United States was covered by forests, estimated to have contained almost eight trillion board feet of lumber, or four times what we have today. From 1700 to 1900, the forests were thought of as endless, and their value was only in conversion to lumber. The philosophy was to "cut it down and get it out." The development of the forest industry as we know it today came fairly late in this period. As late as 1870, three fourths of all standing timber in the United States was publicly owned, but by 1910 four fifths of it was in private holdings.

Despite the "cut it down and get it out" philosophy, during the period of unrestricted clear-cutting, fires still remained the single most destructive agent of the forest. Probably the largest fire in terms of acres of forest destroyed occurred in the early 1900's on the Olympic Peninsula in Washington where over a million acres burned, destroying enough lumber to have supplied the entire nation for a year!

In the late 1800's a concept of forest conservation began to replace the former philosophy of previous generations, and in 1873 Yellowstone was set apart as the first national park in the United States. Today the U.S. national park system includes more than 180 areas totaling nearly 25 million acres. And the national forest system, which is used as a timber reserve and for recreational purposes, includes 180 million more acres.

In the less-developed countries, deforestation is projected to continue until about 2020. By then virtually all the physically accessible forests are expected to have been cut in those nations where 90 percent of the wood consumption goes for cooking and heating. The loss of woodlands will force those people to pay steeply rising prices for fuel wood and charcoal or do without.

According to the *Global 2000 Report,* the most encouraging developments are those associated with heightened international awareness of the seriousness of current trends in world forests. We can do our part by helping campers be aware of the many problems facing the forests and by working hard to improve the woodlands on or near our camps and homes.

As an activity, go for a walk with your campers in a part of the forest. Is it a healthy forest? Why, or why not? What kinds of trees, plants, animals, and birds do you see living in it? Are there others you do not see? Where are they?

Lead a discussion on the factors that might make a forest unhealthy, including such things as disease, pests, fire, drought, wind, pollution, poor soil, floods, and human actions. What suggestions do the campers have of actions people can take to help the forest stay healthy? For example, people can prevent forest fires and remove diseased trees so they will not infect others. What are the short-term and long-term effects of these actions? What if, for example, all fires are prevented in all forests? What happens to trees that depend on certain kinds of fire for regeneration? What purposes do dead trees and brush serve in the forest? They provide homes for animals, birds, and insects, and they eventually decay into the soil to improve its fertility.

Draw a map of the camp's forest, and indicate the different management practices in use, or suggest practices that could be started. Could some of these be done by the campers and camp staff? Invite the local forest ranger or university extension forester to meet with your group for a presentation and to answer questions about local practices and requirements. Ask this person about help in securing the proper kinds of seedlings from the state nursery to start a reforestation project at the camp. This would be a good activity in which to involve all the campers. They could come back for many years to see how "their" trees are developing.

WE SHARE ONE EARTH

The earth on which we live is always changing. The land erodes, winds blow, and water flows in different patterns. Plants, animals, and people live and grow and die. Everything that happens is connected in some way. The height of a mountain influences the amount of rain that will fall nearby. The amount of rainfall influences the amount of erosion and also the kinds of plants that will grow well. This influences the style of life of the people who live by the mountain and how they feel about the earth.

Whatever the changes have been, and no matter where we live, we share one earth with all the plants and animals and other people. And when we start to clean up the water and the air, save wild animals, plant trees, eat less and eat lower on the food chain, we are starting to save the whole earth!

8.
Food Production and Distribution

Humanity has never lived without hunger— it is our oldest and most lethal enemy. Yet for the first time ever you and I face the possibility of ending this age-old fear for everyone on the face of the earth. Agricultural and development experts claim it is self-evident that world hunger can be eradicated by the year 2000. All we lack, they indicate, is the individual and global concern and willpower to take the necessary steps.

Campers who have not yet reached adulthood often have little awareness of the meaning and value of food in their lives in spite of what we adults may believe. Frequently, meal and snack selections lacking in nutrition are made as campers respond to advertising or peer pressure. We see this in purchases at the canteens in some camps, and also when someone at the dining table says, "Ugh, I don't like that!" before even tasting what is being served. Waste is a way of life nowadays, and changes in our North American diet in recent years have contributed to the global food crisis.

FOOD IS IMPORTANT

Food is a very important part of camp! And I can guarantee that no matter how excellent the quality or the quantity of the meals served during your program, you will hear complaints about the food!

But starting with the first meal of your session, you can help campers understand that here is a place where we can try out new foods, experience alternative diets, and put into practice what it means to be faithful stewards of food. Of course, it is incumbent on those of us who administer the program to work cooperatively and supportively with the food service staff to be sure the meals and snacks we serve are consistent with our concerns for good nutrition, fit in with the responsible use of energy and resources, and demonstrate our concern for world hunger issues. By working together, sharing goals and problems, the whole staff will find different and creative ways to involve campers of all ages and from all backgrounds in mealtime learning experiences.

The following objectives can be accomplished in your food-related experience:

1. Campers will use food without wasting it.

2. Campers will develop a willingness to eat new foods and those from different cultures.

3. Campers will gain an understanding of the relationship between their patterns of consumption and global food needs.

4. Campers will learn why they should avoid foods that lack nutritional value or are overpackaged.

5. Campers will develop an understanding of why it is best to eat foods lower on the food chain.

6. Campers will develop a desire to be more involved in the growth and preparation of their food at home.

SETTING UP POSITIVE EXPERIENCES

There are a number of ways in which mealtimes can be made a positive part of the total camp learning program rather than a break from it, or even a negative influence. Here are several things you can try.

Cabins or family groupings sit together. This may not be as natural for some families as you might think, since many families seldom take time to sit down and eat together. Thus, table conversation may not be familiar to some campers either. It is important for counselors to eat with their group, especially if yours is not an intergenerational program but is made up of age groups in cabins.

Eating in a family-type group makes mealtime a great opportunity to evaluate what has been going on, make plans for the next time periods, and talk over any problems.

Serve meals family-style if you can. This means everyone at the table will start eating at the same time and group interaction is stimulated by the simple task of passing dishes from one person to another. Remember that one of our objectives is to get all campers to at least try a bit of everything that is served. To do this requires some guidance and perhaps the suggestion that everyone take and eat at least a spoonful of everything. Actually, some campers will be surprised that they like something that "looks funny" or that they did not think they liked at home.

There are several good ways to reduce the amount of food wasted. One way is to control portions. This means that someone (food server or counselor, usually) will have to provide guidance in the amount of food taken by each camper and particularly by children and youth. A more effective way I have seen is to keep a record of exactly how much is thrown away. This can be done for each table group or for the entire camp. At the end of each meal the wasted food is scraped into a container and weighed. The results may be posted or in some other way reported back to the campers.

By the way, you should be sure that all campers know of your efforts to recycle as much waste as you can. In Chapter 7 we talked about composting and help from your campers during chore time.

It is an unhealthy tradition at many camps to "gobble down" the food as quickly as possible so as to get back to the fun activities. This leads directly to upset stomachs, lack of mealtime conversations, and a very low level of awareness of what is being served or how it might be valuable to the body. I have found that calming background music played in the dining hall will remarkedly lower the general noise level and lengthen the time campers take to eat. Staff members who have been trained in the opportunities to be experienced at mealtimes and who understand the concept of "the teachable moment" can further encourage their campers to eat slowly, using their senses while savoring the meal.

We all know that in many ways counselors and other staff members serve as models for campers. Thus, how the staff reacts to the food served, the type of behavior they demonstrate, and how they relate to one another and to those seated with them will all be important in the total learning program experienced by the campers. In some camps, a relatively large percentage of campers may be from minority cultural backgrounds. The food you normally serve may be foreign to them. You can not only encourage them to try something new but invite them to assist in the preparation of some of their traditional dishes for the entire camp. Do not be surprised if it is much spicier than what you are accustomed to, or if your other campers really get "turned on" by it. You may have to switch your menu halfway through the session.

FOOD-RELATED ACTIVITIES

An Icebreaker. Have your campers stand in a line, one behind the other, all facing the same direction. As you ask the question, they can take one step to the right for choice one and to the left for choice two, stepping back to the single line between each question. Here are some sample questions:

Would you rather have a big breakfast or a little breakfast?

Would you prefer meat and potatoes, or fruit and vegetables?

Would you rather have homemade wheat bread, or white bread from the store?

Would you rather have raisin bran, or a sugar-coated cereal?

Would you prefer eating in a fast-food restaurant, or going on a picnic?

Would you prefer eating some new food, or eating what you are used to?

Make up some questions to suit your campers and your camp situation. When you have asked all the questions, be sure to take time to discuss the various choices and find out why they made them.

Tour the Kitchen. Arrange for a time to visit the kitchen (best when meals are not being prepared and after cleanup is done) and talk with the cooks or the person in charge of food service. Encourage campers to ask such questions as the following:

How much food does the camp use each day? each session? all summer? (Can you get the information on specific items like how many quarts of milk? how many apples? how many boxes of cereal?)

How much does the food cost for each person each day? How much does it cost for labor? for utilities? What other food service costs are there?

How is the menu selected? Where do the recipes come from? Who orders the food?

How much food is wasted each day? What happens to leftovers? What is done with the waste?

Where does the raw food come from? How many hands does it pass through between the field and the dining table?

How have the camp menus changed in the past several years? What influenced the changes?

Pyramid Game. In an open area that is soft to fall on have the campers create a pyramid (usually best with seven campers on the first level, five on the second level, three on the third, and one on the top). Discuss how this shows the interdependence of all levels of life. Compare the pyramid to food sources. For example, plants (vegetables) receive energy directly from the earth, using the chlorophyll in their cells to take the sun's energy and convert the soil's ingredients into nutrients. The next level, plant eaters (animals), get their nutrients by eating the plants. Which have more nutrients, animals or plants? Why? Which have the highest level of chemical buildup? Why? Where are humans on the food pyramid? (On top— we are dependent on the entire food chain.) Why are vegetables good for us? Meat contains valuable protein, but some people live only on vegetables and grains. How is this possible? How might we help the whole world food situation by eating more vegetables and grains and less meat?

Food Montage. Using magazine pictures, make a montage of foods everyone in your group likes. Then make another montage of foods most of the campers do not like. How do they differ? Sit in a circle and discuss your feelings about food. How was it grown and distributed when your grandparents were your age? How is it grown and distributed today? How have these changes affected our eating habits? How many times each week does your family sit down and eat together? Is that important? Why? What are your favorite foods? Where do they come from? How do your eating habits affect people in other parts of the world? How about some people who live near you? What kinds of changes can you make to help others live a better life? How can you help your family understand this and want to change?

You Are What You Eat. The way food is now processed and preserved means that we eat much more than the actual food. Give each of your campers a food package label that includes the ingredients. Tell the campers not to show anyone their label. Then one by one have them read the list of ingredients out loud without naming the food. Have the other campers try to guess what the food is. Afterward ask how many contained some artificial flavoring or coloring. How many contained sugar? For how many was sugar listed as one of the first three ingredients? (Ingredients are listed in the order of the amount present in the food.) What is the purpose of most of the long-word ingredients? (They are added as preservatives.)

The Importance of Whole Grains. Most of the bread and pasta products we eat contain white flour. Ask your campers which they think is better-tasting, white or whole wheat bread. Then ask which is better for you. Milled products—white rice, white flour, cornmeal, and most breakfast cereals—have the germ and bran removed. Whole-grain products use the entire grain. These products include rolled oats, brown rice, popcorn, and puffed grains. Whole-grain products contain far more nutrients because the germ contains most of the food value and the bran has the second largest amount. Whole grains are important to our diet because they have B vitamins, minerals such as iron for our blood, fiber to prevent constipation, and protein.

Eating as if the World Mattered. Eating foods lower on the food chain with good nutrition is good for us and for the entire world! Fewer resources are used in the preparation of natural foods than in processed foods. If we eat more of "our share" of the natural foods and less of the processed, imported foods, there will be more healthy foods for the rest of the world. You can help your campers understand this by staging a hunger fast and not serving one designated meal during the week, and sending the cost of the food not prepared to a world hunger project.

As you prepare for the camp session, watch the newspapers and your denominational publications for articles and figures on the specific effects of government budget changes on food programs. How many elderly people have to choose between buying fuel for heat and food? How has the changing cost of foods such as meat, vegetables, and fruits affected proper nutrition?

Visit agencies that relate to senior citizens. Have food programs been discontinued? Check with the local chapter of the Gray Panthers for information about hunger among the elderly in your area. Check with your local welfare office for instances of hunger among single-parent families and families in which the head of the household is unemployed. Walk through the aisles of a local supermarket to note which sections contain the least nourishing products (for example, the salt and sugar aisles). Talk to someone on your denominational area staff to learn what the church is doing to combat hunger and how you can help.

9.
Healthful Wholeness

Many North Americans have come to believe that medicine and medical technology can solve all our health problems, physical or mental. The role of such important factors as diet, exercise, and even close friends on cancer, heart disease, and depression have long been obscured by our continual emphasis on the miracles of modern medical science. Treatment, not prevention, has been the order of the day.

The problems can never be solved merely by more and more medical care, no matter how excellent it might be. The physical and mental health of an individual, and the health of our whole nation, are determined by several factors, chief among which are the food we eat, the amount of exercise we get, and how we relate to people around us. You really cannot separate these factors; they are a whole, and we will consider them briefly under the general theme of healthful wholeness.

TEMPLE TRIMMERS

Quite literally, you are what you eat. And over the past generation the diet of most Americans has become increasingly rich—rich in meat, rich in other sources of saturated fat and cholesterol, and rich in sugar. According to the U.S. Senate Select Committee on Nutrition and Human Needs, although our total food consumption has fallen, we still eat too much in relation to our actual needs, and the proportion of fatty and cholesterol-rich foods and refined foods in our total diet has risen. The select committee also indicated that we might be better able to tolerate this diet if we were much more active physically.

Worrying about being overweight is one of America's popular pastimes, but worrying alone does not do any good. Medical specialists say that millions of us have genuine cause for concern. Being overweight matters! Excess weight puts more strain on the body, and studies have shown that those who are overweight run a greater risk of serious illness, especially heart and circulatory diseases, certain forms of cancer, and diabetes. They also appear to have less resistance to pneumonia and influenza. There are some indications that overweight people also suffer from gallbladder and liver disorders more frequently than slim people, and statistics prove that overweight people tend to have more accidents.

Health is not the only valid argument for trying not to be overweight. How we appear to others as well as to ourselves is a major factor in determining how happy we will be in life and the kinds of activities in which we participate with any regularity. Campers will be able to understand this at once.

Why do we eat more than we should? Here are some of the primary reasons. If we grasp these reasons, we can help our campers through a positive program throughout the entire session.

1. Most people do not know the caloric value of various foods. A good calorie chart will be helpful as we talk about basic nutrition.

2. A great many people underestimate how much physical activity is required to "work off" the energy value of the food eaten.

3. Some Americans do not know which foods and beverages provide nutrition and which ones add only "empty calories" with little or no nutritional value.

At one camp I visited I read an interesting sign on the dining room wall. It said:

TEMPLE TRIMMERS

We as a staff of one body believe I Corinthians 6:19-20. Our bodies are the temple of the Holy Spirit which should be taken care of for God's glory. As one we join together to lose 140 unneeded pounds. This we do as an act of stewardship for our bodies.

With the sign there was a simple scale, marked from 0 to 140 with a movable pointer. Every day each staff person could add his or her weight loss to the previous total by moving the pointer the appropriate number of pounds.

How many of your campers are the "desirable" weight? Can you begin your own "temple trimmers" club? How can you support one another in a weight loss effort? You will need a good set of scales and a chart of desirable weights for adults and children. Ask your local librarian, a local school nurse, health department, and so on.

Food is an important part of the camping program. Most of us are often unaware, however, of the full impact that mealtime has on campers. Campers learn by example and, for many, the camp staff will be the first live role models they will have experienced outside of the home, school, or church school. In our Bible study programs we talk about our concern for hungry people in our land and around the world, and our concern to keep ourselves physically, mentally, and spiritually fit, but a much deeper lesson can be learned if our own use of daily food demonstrates this concern. The ancient Romans had a slogan that we would do well to adopt: "Facta non verba." Freely translated, this means "deeds, not words."

The "rules of the road" for a balanced, healthy daily diet are quite simple. You do not have to spend a lot of time thinking about whether or not the food you eat is good for you. Many foods contain the elements you need for good health. Unless your physician prescribes a special diet, eating a wide variety of foods is all that is necessary for a well-balanced diet that provides calories for physical activities and nutrients for the body's growth, maintenance, and repair. Be sure that your daily diet includes selections, varied and in moderation, from each of the four basic food groups. Talk with the camp cook if you believe the menu does not take this into account.

Conduct a survey with your campers to determine the group's eating habits. For example, ask them to describe a typical breakfast during the winter (schooltime) months. Where do they eat? With whom? Who prepares the food? Do this for all three meals. Discuss the results. Consider what changes ought to be made.

HEALTH AND FITNESS

You and your campers may have come to the conclusion that people who are carrying around too much weight (that's a polite way of saying "fat") need to go on a diet. But that is only the beginning! Because then you must go after the real problem—how to avoid getting fat all over again. How can you take better care

The Basic Four	
Group	Daily Amounts

Milk Group
  Milk (whole, low-fat, nonfat,
    buttermilk)
  Cheese
  Ice cream
	Adults: 2 cups
	Children: 3–4 cups

Meat Group
  Meat
  Poultry
  Fish
  Eggs
  Dry beans, peas, nuts
	2 or more servings
	Count as one serving:
	  2 or 3 ounces of lean cooked meat,
	    poultry, or fish
	  2 eggs
	  1 cup cooked dry beans or peas
	  4 tablespoons of peanut butter

Vegetable/Fruit Group	4 or more servings
	Count as one serving:
	  ½ cup of vegetables or fruit
	Include:
	  a citrus fruit or vitamin C–rich vegetable
	    daily
	  a leafy green vegetable and a deep
	    yellow vegetable at least every other
	    day

Bread/Cereal Group
  Whole-grain or enriched
	4 or more servings
	Count as one serving:
	  1 slice of bread
	  1 ounce of ready-to-eat cereal
	  ½ to ¾ cup cooked cereal, noodles, rice,
	    etc.

of yourself, changing your body chemistry so that fewer calories are converted to fat?

It is no secret—the ultimate solution to the problem of being fat is exercise. Exercise increases your muscle mass, tones it, and changes its chemistry so that you burn more calories, even when you are asleep!

Anything we do that uses our muscles can be called exercise, and any exercise, even sweeping the cabin floor or picking up litter around the camp, helps to keep our muscles in better shape. But to keep our bodies as fit as they were intended to be, we need exercises that use them.

The word *aerobic* means "air," and refers to the oxygen that is needed by the muscles as they work. The harder the muscles work, the more oxygen they need. Aerobic exercises are steady exercises that require an uninterrupted workout by your muscles over at least a twelve-minute period. As your muscles work aerobically, they get leaner, your heart and lungs increase their capacity to provide oxygen to the muscles, and your body chemistry changes automatically so you burn more fat calories without even knowing it.

Most people claim to have limited time to spend in exercise, and aerobic exercises are the answer here too. Experts who know how to measure such things indicate that you can get as much benefit out of fifteen minutes of jogging as you can out of two hours of strenuous tennis. It is easy to see that for most of us, it is much better to do a steady twelve-minute aerobic exercise every day for conditioning and fat control, and then play tennis for fun!

The main point about aerobic exercise is that it must be steady and continuous for at least twelve minutes. Two six-minute periods of exercise do not add up to aerobics! In fact, some exercises need more than twelve minutes to achieve the same effect because, for the first few minutes, your body (heart, lungs, and muscles) has not reached the training rate.

One of the very best books I know of on this entire subject is Covert Bailey's *Fit or Fat?* For a complete discussion of body fitness, I suggest that you include a copy in the camp library. Included in the book are a number of charts to help you, the staff, and campers to determine your fitness level, percentage of body fat, and at what rate you should exercise.

Find out the kinds of physical exercise your campers participate in regularly and encourage them to continue and increase their exercise while at camp. In our program we include a number of opportunities daily for exercise—hikes, swimming, organized sports, "camp olympics," and so forth. We also encourage campers of all ages who are interested in jogging to join the regular staff joggers on their daily run. With some advance planning we even included youth and adult campers in some of our local races.

FRIENDS CAN BE GOOD MEDICINE

Taking care of your body by watching the kinds and amounts of food you eat is important. Maintaining and improving your fitness level through regular aerobic exercise is also vital. Medical research has only recently begun to demonstrate, however, that supportive personal relationships can help protect both our mental *and* physical health. Plainly stated, this means that friends can be good medicine!

Some of the recent evidence that points toward the importance of supportive relationships in maintaining good physical health include:

- Rates of mental hospitalization are roughly five to ten times greater for separated, divorced, and widowed persons than for married people.
- Socially isolated persons have two to three times more overall risk of dying prematurely than people who are connected with others.
- For older people, having a confidant significantly helps to avoid psychiatric symptoms such as so-called senility.
- Women who have a close friend in whom they confide are less likely to become seriously depressed.
- Terminal cancer strikes divorced individuals of both sexes more frequently than people who are married.

In the face of this new medical research, and in light of the changing times where social ties within families and neighborhoods are far more fragile than in the past, it is extremely vital that we communicate to our intergenerational campers the importance of supportive relationships in maintaining their health. One way to start thinking about friendships and their role in our lives is to answer as a group questions such as these:

What is the nature of a health-promoting relationship? What is the nature of a health-destroying relationship?

What kinds of barriers do we put up against supportive relationships?

Why is it that when we need others the most, we often pull away and withdraw into ourselves?

How can we renew a personal relationship? Give examples.

What can we do at camp to encourage relationships that are health-promoting?

It is not easy to make and keep friends, but the facts are clear: Friends can be good medicine!

WHEN WE NEED SUPPORT THE MOST—AND HOW WE GET IT

In times of crisis such as the death of a loved one, divorce, job loss, personal injury, and major transitions, we need extra support. Most of us have some stress in our everyday lives, and as the stress level goes up, so does our need for support. Stress is very much a part of our lives, and some researchers claim that stress is at the root of from 50 to 80 percent of all diseases. The good news is that supportive friends, family, and groups help protect us from the harmful effects of stress. In fact, there is evidence that their presence even helps reduce stress in our lives by helping us care about ourselves. So although we cannot change our past, during this session at camp we can certainly take the first steps to do something about our future support systems!

There are three basic ways you and your campers can find support when you need or want it:

1. The easiest but not very reliable way—*you simply wait until support is given.* Most of us started out our lives waiting for support, and a great many people still experience a feeling of dependency on others and their judgments. Some people spend their entire lives in this way; their method of controlling their own lives is to give up control to others.

2. The second way is harder but more reliable—*you simply ask for support.* Unfortunately, many of us are afraid to ask. It may be that we do not want to risk the rejection that might come. We might feel embarrassed, thinking that asking for support is a sign of weakness or that we lack certain skills. Or we may be silenced by our own shyness.

3. The third way may be the hardest but it is the surest way—*you simply give support,* and you get support in return. Most experienced support givers agree that the giver receives more from the act of giving than the receiver gets. Remember that Jesus said, "Give to others, and God will give to you. . . . You will receive a full measure, a generous helping, poured into your hands—all that you can hold. The measure you use for others is the one that God will use for you." *(Luke 6:38.)* And Paul quoted Jesus, saying, "There is more happiness in giving than in receiving." *(Acts 20:35.)*

Giving feels good immediately because it gives us a feeling of self-worth and self-esteem. Counselors tell us that self-esteem is a key ingredient in self-care, which leads to healthy wholeness. It will also give you and your campers courage to ask for supportive help when you need it as well as the power to change your lives and to manage your own affairs in relation to others.

There are some real obstacles to making and maintaining friendships and other support systems. These include time limitation, compromises, and the emotional costs of relationships. Distance does not need to be a barrier. Compared to the artificial barriers that get in the way of developing or nurturing a strong relationship, the real barriers are relatively few in number. Artificial barriers include the following:

1. Shyness. Almost half of the American people consider themselves shy, and this prevents a great many people from doing what they want to do and relating with others the way they would like to relate.

2. Fear. Many of us are overly anxious about the unknown, and many people are so afraid of failure that they never attempt anything new, including trying to be a friend to a stranger or a coworker.

3. Labeling. We classify people and then always see them through these labels. This excludes a lot of people as potential friends and supporters.

4. Pride, macho image, distinct and past negative experiences. These also get in the way of establishing and maintaining friendships.

The critical fact is that it is best not to wait for a crisis to suddenly begin looking to others for support. Someone once said, "Friends don't come for free" to explain that the hardest part of having friends is being a friend, which takes time and effort. But long-time cultivation and expending of time and concern with friends is a benefit to our health and theirs.

With your campers discuss what it means to be a good friend. *Proverbs 17:17* tells us, "Friends always show their love. What are brothers for if not to share trouble?" And in *John 15:13* Jesus said, "The greatest love a person can have for his friends is to give his life for them." What are the qualities of friends? Here are some starter ideas:

Friends keep confidences (they do not tell the other's secrets!).

Friends are loyal to one another.

Friends share warmth and affection.

Friends tell the truth, frankly, to one another.

Friends are sensitive to each other's feelings.

Friends share feelings.

Friends share their sense of humor.

Friends do not talk all the time—sometimes they listen!

Friends help each other resolve personal and interpersonal conflicts.

Friends are committed; they stay in touch.

Talk with your campers about ways you can deepen the friendships being established during this session at camp. What can each of you do to help friendship develop and deepen? How can you nourish it even when you leave camp? For example, you can take time to talk with one another, to really communicate, to learn what is important to each of you—your hobbies, your interests, your work, your families, your concerns, your fears, your dreams. You can share gifts with one another that cost little or no money—a note, a flower, an article or picture from a magazine, a poem, a story, a joke, or a song. When you leave camp you can write a note, send a birthday greeting, or make a telephone call.

WELLNESS

Many corporations in America now offer "wellness programs" to their employees. They recognize that an improved life-style reduces absenteeism, increases productivity, decreases health insurance costs, and improves morale. Branches of our federal and state governments are working toward health education and controls over harmful substances.

As individuals who are trying to be faithful stewards of all God's creation, how shall we live? We remember that we were created in God's image *(Gen. 1:26-27)*, although the Fall caused us to lose that spiritual likeness. But the New Testament urges us to "put on the new self" *(Eph. 4:22-24)*, and reminds us that our body is the temple of the Holy Spirit *(I Cor. 6:19-20)*. Therefore we ought to strive to maintain a personal stewardship program that gives us a wholesome life-style, remembering that Almighty God has promised to provide us with all that we need for this life *(John 14:27; Matt. 6:33; Rom., ch. 8)*.

We know that our body needs regular rest. Paul used the symbolism of physical conditioning to show spiritual perseverance *(I Cor. 9:24-27)*. Regular and balanced meals, eaten in moderation, avoiding high fat content and including fiber foods, are of great benefit. Our bodies do belong to the Lord *(I Cor. 6:13)* and we must take care of them for God.

In addition to doing what is right, we can actively resist what is bad for us. We can stop smoking. Recent tests prove there is no safe level of smoking! Alcohol should be kept to a minimum. According to all research, there are no known deficiency diseases due to a lack of alcohol. Most of us already regard illicit drugs as poison to the body and the mind.

There is one final commitment to stewardship of the body that I pray each one of you will seriously consider. The wonderful God-given body that you occupy during this earthly pilgrimage will eventually return to the soil from which you were formed *(Gen. 3:19)*. As an additional and final act of stewardship, you can will your organs for transplantation, extending life for someone beyond your death.

10.
Energy Conservation and Production

Fateful choices face the citizens of the world during the next few years in the area of energy. For example, the *Global 2000 Report*'s energy projections show no relief from the already existing "crunch," and point out that the world's petroleum production capacity is not increasing as rapidly as demand, and production will peak before the end of this century. It is very clear that a shift in world dependency must take place away from petroleum, but there is a great deal of uncertainty as to how this transition can and will occur.

Although prices for oil and other commercial energy sources are rising, fuel wood, the poor person's fuel, is expected to become far less available than it is now. In fact, it is projected that, by 1994, 25 percent of the people of the world who depend on fuel wood for cooking and essential heating will not be able to find or afford it. Scarcities are now local but expanding. In some less-developed nations, fuel wood–gathering already has become a full-time job requiring 360 person-days of work per household each year. In some urban areas, which are too far from collectible wood, families spend up to 30 percent of their income for fuel wood. It is easy to understand that this causes deforestation, which is a prime cause of soil loss through erosion.

In Somalia on the east coast of Africa, Christian relief workers have introduced a new stove made from clay and sand, which has already proven that much wood can be saved. In this land of many refugees, residents are being taught how to make the stoves and then to share their new skill with others.

Women, who are traditionally the gatherers of firewood and the cooks in Somalia as well as most other less-developed nations, gain the most from the improved stoves. As forests recede, they must walk longer distances to find twigs and branches needed to cook meals. Fuel-efficient stoves reduce the number of long, fatiguing trips and save women time and energy that can be used to care for their children, tend the fields, and also plant new trees.

In many places where there is little or no wood, and the high cost makes it impossible for people to use it for fuel, growing amounts of dung and crop residues are shifted away from the fields to the cooking fires. It is estimated that worldwide, nearly 400 million tons of dung are burned each year for fuel! We have already pointed out that dung and crop wastes are necessary additions to the soil to replace nutrients and to aid in holding moisture. For the poor, these organic materials are the only source of fertilizer, needed to maintain the productivity of their farmlands. These nutrients will be urgently needed for food production in the years ahead, since by the year 2000 the world's croplands will have to feed half again as many people as in 1975.

Energy is a social issue that involves facts and values. Unfortunately, although there is an abundant supply of facts, many of them are in conflict with each other. And energy values are often a jumble of assumptions about what risks a nation should take, human rights and freedom, equity, and who should make decisions. For those campers who need the practical aspect so they can get into the discussion, point out how utility bills have increased in the past few years. Ask your group to consider how we are going to be able to afford energy for our homes and businesses in the years ahead. Remember, too, that the energy situation is approaching a critical stage for most camps, particularly those trying to switch from summer-only use to year-round operation with inadequate facilities, because energy costs are projected to continue to rise dramatically in the next twenty years. In fact, considering available supplies, inflation, and production and distribution costs, most energy experts estimate that for every $100 we spend now for energy, we will spend over $800 in 2000!

CONSERVATION

The possibility of using energy more efficiently—making conservation an energy source—has gained considerable support in our country after other alternatives have been considered. It has been estimated that about half of the energy in North America could be saved, if we were really serious about it, without adversely affecting our health or happiness. The largest savings can be made in the areas of transportation, buildings, industrial use, electricity generation, and energy recovery from waste. Conservation is an attitude that is open to all of us, can be fully demonstrated, discussed, and learned at an integenerational camp, and can be translated into the home, school, and work situation during the rest of the year.

For most of us, to conserve means to make a change in life-style. We have already seen that the average life-style in North America is pretty energy-intensive. By this we mean that although we have about 6.5 percent of the world's population, we consume 38 percent of the world's commercially produced energy. To put it plainly, we are used to flipping a switch to turn on a light and then leaving it on when we leave the area; in our homes we regularly heat rooms that are not occupied; and without thinking we drive our large automobiles two blocks to pick up one small package of processed food. Life-style changes, however, whether corporate or individual, are usually met with considerable resistance, so we need to be prepared for this in our campers as well as in ourselves. By the way, you may be surprised to learn that industry has a much better track record in energy conservation—if not in advertising that promotes the use of energy—than most of the rest of us (to say nothing about the institutional church).

I started out to describe sixty-eight ways to conserve energy around camp and home. Instead, however, I will simply refer you to your local power company and other agencies. At your local library you may find (at 644 in the Dewey Decimal System) a shelf-long collection of energy conservation books such as *Energy-saving Projects You Can Build,* by the editors of *Better Homes and Gardens,* 1979, and *Energy Alternatives,* produced by Time-Life Books, 1982. Some others are listed in the Bibliography. You and your campers should discuss at length all the energy-saving ideas you can find.

ENERGY GENERATION

We have said that conserving energy calls for a change in life-style for most of us. Many of us are already changing the way we live so that we can conserve, and we will be making more changes in the years to come. Now I want to suggest another change—a change from being just a consumer of energy to being a producer also. Here is information about several power sources. Some of them could be used to generate energy at camp. Be sure to stress several points:

1. These are just ideas—you should check your local library for detailed plans and technological advice.

2. Since these are just ideas, they can be modified by a creative-minded person into something much better.

3. There is always some danger in any project, and these should not be attempted by children or inexperienced youth alone. Rather, this is a good way to involve some older adults who perhaps have had years of experience in the construction trades and can share their knowledge and skills.

Water Power

Many camps have at least one stream on their site; yet the idea that even a small stream can provide a useful source of power has never occurred to most camp directors. Or if it did, the idea has been rejected as too difficult or expensive to accomplish. The fact remains, however, that some pretty impressive advantages can be had from a small water-power installation.

Electricity can be generated for demonstration purposes if nothing else. And the pond that is usually created can serve additionally as a reservoir for firefighting, as a swimming pool, or as a fishing pond. If you live where it gets cold enough for water to freeze, you can ice-skate on it!

Electric power can be generated from just about any flowing stream, no matter how small. Whether or not it is desirable to harness the power depends on two factors. First, does the water flow all year (or at least in the summer months when camp is in operation)? Second, does enough water flow to make a generator installation economically worthwhile? Of course, if you are interested in a demonstration project you may not need to ask what is the least amount of electric power that is worth developing. From a commercial standpoint, at least one waterwheel manufacturer produces a series of small-capacity hydroelectric units, down to 500-watts size. This is enough electricity to light ten fair-sized lamps or to operate a ⅔-horsepower pump.

Building and installing a complete hydroelectric generator in one week would be very difficult. However, your campers can get the idea of the force available by making small waterwheels and flow-testing them by holding them in the stream current. You can experiment with different kinds of wheels; having the water flow over a wheel, under it, or beside it; creating a dam and using water that "falls" from the top of the dam (thus getting greater pressure); and so forth. As a variation of water power, *carefully* hold the waterwheel in the steam coming from a boiling tea kettle. What are the advantages of steam power? of water power? What kind of water or steam generators do your nearby utility companies use? What is the fuel? What kind of spiritual lessons can we learn from hydroelectric generators?

Underwater Generators. For centuries people have tried to harness the energy of the sea, using exotic methods such as "wave machines." Now, it turns out, some energy-hungry regions may have a clean, inexpensive, easily accessible system for generating electricity using the rapidly churning waters of the ocean. Researchers have devised an underwater turbine that can take advantage of the ocean's perpetually strong currents (up to 7.5 feet per second in some places!). Equipped with blades like a child's pinwheel, the underwater generator would be anchored to the sea bottom where the force of moving water will spin its propellers and generate electricity that can be channeled ashore without appreciable environmental impact.

Although the expense of installing several hundred turbines, each 300 feet long, might seem prohibitive, oceanic turbines are actually a remarkably frugal system. Maintenance expenses would be low since the turbine can be anchored for up to a year before being floated to the surface for inspection and cleaning. And some economists claim each unit would begin to show a profit in fourteen months, compared to a nuclear plant which does not begin to show a profit for ten years.

Cold Power. Together, all the earth's rivers and inland lakes contain about 125,000 cubic kilometers of fresh water. What if many times this amount existed in a single area and could be used for hydroelectric power? It does, and engineers say it can be! The Greenland ice cap holds in icy bondage almost twenty times as much fresh water as is found in all the lakes and rivers on earth combined! And although this vast resource is frozen most of the year, in the summer months much of it thaws, pouring in torrents onto nearby lowlands. Scientists at the United Nations Institute for Training and Research are studying the possibility of harnessing this energy to run hydroelectric turbines.

Transmitting the electrical power through a system of undersea cables would be possible, but there would be a 20 percent loss of voltage. Instead, the electric power could be used at full power in Greenland to convert water into hydrogen, which then could be transported as a liquid by tankers to be used as a fuel.

Wind Power

More and more utility companies are experimenting with wind generators, and you can too. You should remember, however, that your success depends to a large degree on your camp's location. It may be in a sheltered spot where you do not normally get much wind. If this is true, then no matter how fancy or expensive a unit you build, you probably will not get much power.

When you start dreaming of wind power for your home or camp, be mindful of these two basic routes to follow: you can choose a modest machine producing direct current to charge a bank of batteries; or you can select a larger, higher-output alternating current unit with a powerline tie-in. Feeding batteries with a small wind machine allows you to accumulate power when you do not need it. Using a line tie-in is somewhat like putting electricity in the power company's energy bank.

The intermittent nature of wind as an energy source makes it most useful in applications in which the electricity can be stored in batteries. And this means that if you are going to depend on your own power, you had better be prepared for "blackouts." There are some commercial wind generators on the market, but they are still quite expensive. So for the time being I would advise you just to familiarize your campers with the idea of wind power. Make some windmill models. How many blades work best in the spinner? (Three, because you cannot balance one blade, two blades will have vibration problems, and the addition of a fourth blade will start to slow the spinner down.) What special problems for a wind generator would be caused by various amounts of wind (from zero miles per hour to gale force)? Are there places on the campsite that might be appropriate for a wind generator? Are there any wind generators installed near the camp that you and your campers might visit? What is your local utility company doing in regard to wind generation of energy?

Sailing Ships. Most of us think of large ships with masts and sails as something romantic out of the past. But in Germany and Japan—two nations with an acute need to conserve imported oil—prototypes have been built of what may be a new fleet of sail-aided cargo ships. Developers say that with a 30-knot wind abeam, the sails on the fully loaded ships can provide 53 percent of the power needed to travel at 12 knots. As every sailor and kite flyer knows, winds constantly shift in direction and vary in speed. To get the most power from the wind at sea, a microcomputer system gives automatic commands to small electric motors to turn the steel-framed canvas sails by rotating the masts. In a fair or strong wind, the engines slow down automatically to work no harder than necessary to maintain constant speed. The designers claim that fuel savings can be as high as 50 percent!

Canadian Projects. Work by the National Research Council has given Canada a lead in the development of the vertical-axis wind turbine, which employs an "eggbeater" rotor configuration. During the early 1980's, a number of field trials of small wind machines for remote sites were carried out on Prince Edward Island.

The largest wind machine presently in operation in Canada is the 40-meter high, 230-kilowatt (kw) wind turbine generator in the Magdalen Islands. A decision was recently made by the federal government to construct a similar but larger machine. Called Project Aeolus, this wind turbine will supply enough electrical energy to provide for the nonheating needs of six hundred households.

Biomass Power

Here is a project you can build and operate within a one-week session, assuming that all the parts are available. Biomass generation refers to the generation of gas that can be burned for cooking or to boil water to make steam or to operate a gas engine. In this particular project, enough methane gas can be generated with this digester to cook a one-course meal each day. Someone in the group should have basic soldering skills for the construction of the digester. And since the methane gas generated by the digester is inflammable (and if mixed accidentally with air, is *explosive*), it is vital that mature adult supervision be provided at all times.

The cost of materials will be minimal, especially if you are able to recycle some of them from the camp maintenance department.

Here is the procedure. Be sure to study the illustration carefully for details. You will see that there are just three basic parts to this digester: (1) a fifty-five-gallon drum to hold the manure slurry, (2) an inner tube from a truck tire to store the methane gas, and (3) a gate valve for regulating the flow of gas.

The chief function of the digester is to hold a manure slurry out of contact with oxygen. This allows the anaerobic digestion of the manure to take place. The bacteria that decompose the manure slurry produce methane gas as a by-product. Yes, this is very similar to our compost bin described earlier. But in this case it is important to emphasize that the decomposition of the manure must take place in the absence of oxygen, otherwise methane will not be produced. So if you want the digester to work as it should, it must be airtight!

The fifty-five-gallon drum used for this digester should have a screw plug which will allow the addition of manure slurry or the emptying of slurry that is used up. The galvanized steel piping and gate valve, which you will see in the illustration, must be soldered to the drum just like soldering water piping. An inner tube from a truck tire is used to store the methane gas, and the hose used to connect the inner tube to the galvanized pipe can be sealed to the tire with silicon glue.

You will see that when the gate valve is closed, the methane gas fills the inner tube, and when the gate valve is opened, the stored methane gas is forced out to a burner. A Bunsen burner can be used, or a Coleman stove, but in both cases the adapter (hole) that mixes the air with the gas must be enlarged to allow more air to mix with the low-pressure methane gas.

People who use this kind of digester claim that once it is operational, it will produce about ten cubic feet of methane gas every day, enough to run the burner for about half an hour. The digester will continue to produce methane gas for nearly a month on one filling of manure slurry.

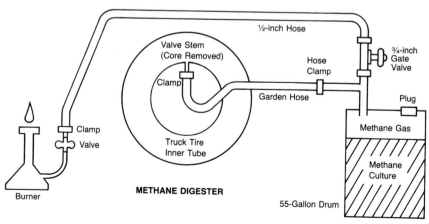

METHANE DIGESTER

CAUTION: Methane is highly volatile if and when mixed with air. Therefore, you must take extreme care to purge the entire system of air before you try to burn the methane. If you have any questions whatsoever about purging the system, check with your local van gas dealer. Once the methane starts to be produced, some of the gas should be allowed to escape into the air. After three or four days, the methane can be checked by a mature adult by bubbling it through water and lighting the gas bubbles with a match. If the gas burns slowly, it is ready to use. But if it lights with a popping sound, you must allow the digester to purge itself for another day or two.

Two factors that greatly influence the amount of methane gas your digester will produce are (1) the temperature of the slurry (95° F. will give optimum results) and (2) the carbon-to-nitrogen ratio of the slurry. The experts say that a slurry containing about thirty times as much carbon as nitrogen will work best. You can get this ratio by mixing organic materials high in carbon (like grass cuttings and leaves) with organic materials that are high in nitrogen (like fresh horse, cow, or chicken manure).

When you are beginning from scratch, it will take up to eight weeks of "culturation" time for the bacteria to start working. You can speed up the process at camp by bringing a jug of "starter" with you from home. This "starter" is simply a small amount of manure slurry, usually about five gallons, which is already rich in the methane-producing bacteria. You can use one five-gallon jug, or five one-gallon jugs. They must have small necks. Place some manure slurry in each bottle and fasten a large balloon over the neck of the bottle. Then let the slurry sit for about eight weeks. As methane gas is produced, it will flow into and expand the balloon. If you plan it properly, the "starter" slurry will be producing methane just about the time the construction of the digester at camp is completed. By adding the "starter" to the manure slurry in the fifty-five-gallon drum, the digester should begin generating methane gas within four days. So by the end of the week you can be cooking with gas!

Geothermal Energy

Two-thousand-year-old Roman documents tell of a valley of steam vents west of what is now Florence, Italy. Starting in the nineteenth century this natural steam was harnessed for heating and mechanical power, and, later, for the generation of electricity. Today, Italy can produce more than 400,000 kilowatts of geothermal electricity. New Zealand, Russia, Japan, Iceland, Mexico, and the Philippines also are using geothermal power. In the United States, two small demonstration power plants began operation in 1920, and the first commercial geothermal unit was put "on-line" in 1960. The Canadian government and British Columbia Hydro are drilling at Meager Mountain, north of Vancouver, to assess the feasibility of building a geothermal electric power station there. More than fifty other nations are considering development of their geothermal resources.

To understand the potential of geothermal energy, it helps to know what is happening beneath the surface of the earth. Down there, usually twenty miles or more beneath the earth's crust, is a mass of molten rock called "magma." However, in a few areas of the earth, particularly around the rim of the Pacific Ocean, magma is found relatively close to the surface, perhaps only five miles or so. In such spots, magma heats the layers of rock above it. If underground water is present, it will begin to boil and will sometimes rise to the surface as hot springs, steam geysers, or fumaroles (openings in the surface, usually in a volcanic area).

When the steam reaches the surface it is first cleansed of tiny rock particles that could damage turbine blades. This is done by "whirling" the particles off in centrifugal separators. Then the steam flows through insulated pipes to the generating units. Spent steam passes to a condenser where it is cooled and becomes water. For campers or staff who are technically minded or may want to build a geothermal unit at camp, let me add that it usually requires a steam well to be dug (average depth, 8,500 feet). Steam is supplied to the turbines at 355° F. and at 100 pounds per square inch pressure.

Geothermal power has many environmental advantages. As fossil fuels diminish in supply and soar in cost, geothermal provides an alternative form of energy. No combustion products are emitted to contribute to smog or acid rain. And no rivers need to be dammed.

Coal—the "Bridge to the Future"?

Coal is the most plentiful fossil fuel in the world and now has the potential for filling an ever-growing share of the need for energy. But there are problems that plague this promising old fuel. For example, the *Global 2000 Report* indicates that much of the energy obtained by burning coal is used to generate electricity, but in the process approximately two thirds of the energy is lost as waste heat.

Coal has been found in most of the developed nations of the world and in some of the less-developed ones as well. Of all known coal reserves, nearly two thirds are in the Soviet Union, China, or North America. At the present rate of consumption, these reserves will last the world more than two hundred years, according to conservative estimates. In addition, some geologists believe the earth probably has fifteen times this much undiscovered coal. Unfortunately, most of this undiscovered coal is not accessible with our present technology or at the present prices. In 1979 the Canadian coal reserves were estimated to be 16.8 billion tons of bituminous coal, 30 billion tons of subbituminous coal, and 3.6 billion tons of lignitic coal.

To produce and use substantially more coal than we do in the world today, a number of problems will have to be solved: shortages of working capital (especially in less-developed nations); labor force and declining productivity; transportation from the mine to the point of use; and environmental concerns such as the proper reclamation of mine sites, potential changes in global climate caused by increased carbon dioxide from burning coal, and the other emissions that form acid rain, erode buildings, poison lakes and forests, and damage the lungs of humans and other living things.

Oil—"Black Gold"

In 1980, the United States consumed more than 15 million barrels of oil a day to provide transportation, heat buildings, drive industry, and provide raw materials for petrochemicals. Of this immense flow, only about 9 million barrels a day came from its own domestic wells. The rest had to be imported, even though the United States is the third largest producer of oil in the world, ranking behind the Soviet Union and Saudi Arabia.

It has been estimated that the United States has about 150 billion barrels of oil in recoverable reserves, using conventional methods of production. At current production rates, this amount will last only nine years, and most experts fear that few major oil fields remain to be found. This makes imported oil all the more important in the way we practice our stewardship of creation. But our dependence on imports is much less than that of Europe, and it is practically nothing compared to oil-poor Japan, whose industrial economy must be fed by a string of tankers arriving at a rate of four a day from foreign sources.

Discoveries of significant new fields, dramatic improvements in the methods of producing oil from currently operating wells, further developments in recovering oil from tar sands and oil shale, and the liquification of coal will be needed very soon unless Americans learn to live on far less or on something completely different!

In Canada the story is somewhat different because there are already excellent possibilities for switching from oil to alternative sources of energy, including coal, uranium, wood, hydroelectricity, and especially natural gas.

To meet the broad challenge of energy in a national framework, Canada instituted the National Energy Program (NEP) in 1980. Already a slight decline in oil product demand has been noted, and this trend is predicted to become more pronounced as the NEP establishes more programs of conservation and substitution. It has been predicted that by 1990 Canadian oil demands will decline to 234 thousand cubic meters per day, whereas production will be 242 thousand cubic meters per day. A cubic meter is the equivalent of 6.29 U.S. barrels.

Natural Gas

With 13 percent of the world's known natural gas reserves, this clean, convenient, and, up to now, inexpensive source has provided 26 percent of North America's energy needs. However, we have consumed 20 trillion cubic feet of gas each year, far outstripping discoveries of new sources, and making many experts believe natural gas is a slowly dwindling resource.

There have been several new gas field discoveries recently, especially in Mexico and Canada. Other advances and proposals include shipment of liquified natural gas from Indonesia and some Arab countries, the construction of a pipeline from Alaska, and the expensive process of coal gasification.

Most analysts predict little increase in our gas supplies during the remainder of this century, and it is clear that here, too, alternative sources of clean, convenient, and cheap energy must be developed by the year 2000.

Making Energy with Nuclear Fission

In any steam-electric power plant, heat boils water to make steam, which turns a turbine generator to make electricity. In most existing power plants, oil, coal, or natural gas is burned to make the steam. In a nuclear fission power plant, heat comes from a nuclear reactor whose fuel is uranium, formed into small, cylindrical pellets and sealed in long metal tubes. Nuclear fission occurs inside the fuel pellets when billions of atoms are split by neutrons—particles of matter even smaller than atoms—and give up their energy to create heat.

Following the highly publicized nuclear accident at Three Mile Island in Pennsylvania in 1979, public attention was all the more focused on this energy source and its radioactive fuel. More recently, there have been major demonstrations against the use of existing nuclear power plants or the construction of new ones. The list of reasons not to use nuclear fission is long and includes the following:

The spent fuel contains plutonium, which is exceedingly toxic, capable of causing cancer in those exposed to it.

The toxic radiation remains deadly for a minimum of tens of thousands of years (the half-life is 24,000 years!)

There is no safe way to transport or store the waste—it will be dangerous for hundreds of generations.

Radioactive materials can (and do) escape into the air from leaks in the power plant systems.

Unknown tragedies could occur as a result of earthquakes, wars, or civil insurrection.

Only 10 to 20 pounds of plutonium is needed to make an atomic bomb, the creation of which is within the technical and financial capacity of many nations and, potentially, political groups or individuals.

With nuclear energy, as with many other fuel alternatives, the raw materials and technology are already at hand. The question is not can we, but should we?

Solar Energy: Ours for the Taking

The sun has been bathing the earth in a torrent of free fusion energy for about six billion years, and it is likely to continue for at least another eight billion. Since the time of Creation, people have been using this solar energy, if only by standing in the sunlight to get warm.

Early in time our ancestors learned to build their huts with a southern exposure so they would receive the sun's warming rays. They found that crops grew better in the sunlight, and animal pelts for clothing—and later the family wash—could be dried by solar power. Now we know, too, that the winds and waterpower used to power sailing ships, windmills, and waterwheels are created by the action of the sun.

Every year the sun drenches North America with five hundred times more energy than we consume, and experts agree that if we could tap only a tenth of that, our entire energy demand could be met with the rays striking just 2 percent of the surface area.

The abundance of inexpensive fossil fuel lulled the energy industry and the Federal Government into ignoring this clean, safe, economical, and virtually inexhaustible source of energy. But now both the Canadian and United States governments have taken major steps to investigate and promote solar usage. For example, about 32 percent of Canada's energy demand is in the form of low-grade heat below 100°C., the majority of it to heat water or space for industrial or residential application. It has been demonstrated that much of this demand could be met by solar energy. To encourage solar usage in the commercial and industrial sectors, solar heating systems are now eligible for a two-year write-off against corporate income. In addition, the Canadian government has spent in excess of $10 million for research and development and has opened a national solar test facility in Mississauga, Ontario.

Some solar devices use concentrators (like the antenna dish on a radar set) to reflect sunlight striking a large area onto a smaller surface, which gets hot enough to boil water or other liquids and create steam to generate electricity. The concentrator usually tracks the sun continually in order to stay in direct sunlight. Production is limited by intermittent clouds, and the system shuts down at night or when the sky is overcast.

Solar energy is also used to heat water or air in flatplate collectors, which normally face southward on rooftops. The hot water can be used for household needs. At one of our camps, twenty-six low-limit flatplate collectors heat the swimming pool water easily to a comfortable 82° F. In so-called active solar systems, solar-warmed air can heat buildings when aided by pumps and fans. Water for many industrial processes can also be heated with this type of collector.

Windows, greenhouses, and other forms of passive solar architecture require no mechanical systems but will admit solar radiation that is absorbed into a building and converted to heat. Even in the far North the sun can warm a building significantly if enough insulation is used to retain the heat.

Solar electric cells, called photovoltaic cells, can generate a considerable amount of electricity when situated for maximum exposure to direct solar radiation. As with all other solar systems, the energy produced depends on changes in the cloud cover, day to day and season to season. For this reason, most solar cell electric systems are connected to large banks of storage batteries so that electric energy will be available on dark days and at night.

In late 1982, researchers announced a breakthrough in the attempt to produce hydrogen from water using direct solar radiation. The hydrogen can be used as fuel in a conventional electric generating plant.

Some people are now saying that in the United States solar programs could meet even more of our energy needs than the official goal of 20 percent by the year 2000.

With your campers, tour the campsite to determine what uses of solar energy are already being made, like southern exposures for buildings, outside clotheslines, and heat for the pool. Make up a list of possible solar additions, including heating domestic water and building heat.

An interesting project we built at camp is a solar oven. The Mother Earth News *Handbook of Homemade Power* (published by Bantam Books, 1974) has an excellent article and plans for building and using a solar oven. One of our ovens is used constantly at a primitive site. The interior reaches over 360° F. with no problem. The same book also contains plans for building a solar water heater that will provide many showers at a remote campsite. Both of these projects can be built in the free time during one week at camp.

Waste Heat: an Overlooked Energy Source

Around most large factories there is a lot of waste heat. For example, we have already mentioned that about two thirds of the energy obtained by burning coal to make steam to generate electricity is lost as waste heat. Around most camps there is waste heat, also.

The problem is how to tap this source of energy to use it inexpensively. Some new products to do just this are now being developed. For example, we are investigating a way to use the heat exhausted by our walk-in freezer compressor to preheat water for the kitchen. Every degree we can raise the water temperature using waste heat is a degree of heat the regular hot water heater will not need to supply! I know a retreat center that preheats kitchen water with the steaming hot waste rinse water from the commercial dishwashing machine by using a simple set of coils of pipe around a central pipe. Many old-timers can remember heating water by running pipes through a woodstove or fireplace. What sources of waste heat can you locate at your camp that can be used for other purposes?

Matter as the Ultimate Fuel

For nearly half a century scientists have known how to unleash massive amounts of energy in the same way the sun does: by nuclear fusion. But for just as long the ability to channel this energy into something besides thermonuclear bombs has escaped them. Finally, research on clean, peaceful fusion has reached a critical time, and optimistic physicists say that they will soon be able to create significant fusion energy for peaceful purposes.

Unlike already existing nuclear energy plants, which produce energy by shattering atoms and leaving behind radioactive waste, fusion plants will copy the sun by welding together simple nuclei without producing dangerous residue. This is not an easy task because the system must heat heavy forms of hydrogen to 180 million degrees Fahrenheit, about six times the temperature of the sun's interior. Energy is released when the atoms' nuclei collide and combine to form a helium nucleus, which weighs slightly less than the total of the individual particles that have merged to form it. The slight mass difference is converted to pure energy, according to Einstein's formula $E = mc^2$.

So far, the scientists have used more energy heating the ionized gas than the resulting fusion has released, and no one yet has devised a means to convert the released energy into a form that can be easily used. So it may not be until the next century that fusion plants can supply commercially available electric power.

Synthetic Fuels

Methanol (wood alcohol), long used as race-car fuel, has been tested for use in airplanes and, unlike fossil fuel, can be produced by industry from just about anything that grows. Other candidates to replace gasoline and kerosene are synfuels made from coal or oil shale. Most scientists do not expect large-scale synfuel production until around the year 2000.

Seawater, or even dirty rainwater, can be transmuted into fuel through a new technique serendipitously discovered by a researcher in medical electronics. The technique involves splitting water molecules by tuning in on the vibrations of their atoms and breaking the molecules into hydrogen, which could be used for fuel, and oxygen. More recent research has shown that similar splitting can be accomplished using a new solar system, which, researchers claim, will provide hydrogen inexpensively enough to be used conveniently in fuel cells or hydrogen-powered cars. Others point out that liquid hydrogen is very explosive and would have to be handled in huge, well-insulated tanks kept at less than $-450°$ F. But hydrogen burns very cleanly, leaving relatively little pollution, and recent government studies indicate that storage and handling problems should not be insurmountable.

11.
Peace and Justice:
Companions for the Journey

Jesus said and did a lot of things that were pretty radical in his day! For example, he once said, "You have heard that it was said, 'Love your friends, hate your enemies.' But now I tell you: love your enemies and pray for those who persecute you. . . ." (*Matt. 5:43-44.*)

It seems to me that this is a good place to begin our brief discussion of peace and justice, two parts of the same big issue that looms up in the face of those who are striving to be good and faithful stewards of creation. It also seems that the key word here is *love.* If we Christians are going to take seriously the asseveration that this simple statement contains the answer to one of humankind's most basic questions, we need to ponder carefully its full implication. I think we can gain insight into the true meaning of what Jesus said by looking at various fairly common uses of the word "love."

First, consider what we mean when we talk about falling in love. How would you or your campers describe that experience? For the time being, remove from consideration the purely physical, biological, sexual aspects of love, without discounting in any way the very important role these aspects play in love. In a great deal of our common use of the word "love," these aspects are given such a prominent place that for many people love is thought to include nothing else of real importance. But many can testify that as significant as they are, these are not the most important aspects of love.

Sometime in the past I remember one of my instructors making a generalized statement like "Love involves a feeling response to perceived value." In other words, we certainly see some kind of value in anything or anyone we say we love. Of course, our perception may be inaccurate or distorted. How well I recall my parents reminding me that "love is blind"! But whatever the case, it is this perception, which helps us see value in the person or object, that causes the feeling response. And so this is the basic starting point for understanding the word and the wonderful experience of loving.

A second consideration is to be aware that we usually associate the idea of acceptance with the act of loving. Acceptance means to receive someone or something willingly and favorably without rejection or resistance. In our relationship with other people it means taking them as they are! Jesus would say that if love is to have its full meaning, then total and unreserved acceptance must be included. And today we can say that if you still love after seeing faults in your beloved, yours is not "blind love."

A third very important—yes, even essential—ingredient of love is a deep concern for the protection, preservation, and enhancement of the values perceived in the object of that love. This concern can be seen in a lover's genuine sacrificial attitude, a complete willingness to lay down his or her life if necessary to ensure the well-being of the beloved.

Can you see how this applies to other people and the environment? I pray that you can. Otherwise, it will be difficult if not impossible for you to be a faithful steward of creation, and what we say next concerning peace and justice issues will not make any sense at all.

I think the most difficult concept Jesus proposed in his simple statement was to love your enemy. What he was saying is to see value in someone who hates you; to fully accept someone who can say nothing good about you; to desire to protect, preserve, and enhance someone who would like to do away with you! This is what love is all about when we talk about peace and justice issues. And, yes, Jesus did understand that of all people, one's enemy is the most difficult to really love.

Elsewhere in his teachings, Jesus stressed the importance of forgiveness toward and prayer for your enemy. As stewards, we should follow our Master's example, set for us on the cross, and forgive those who persecute us. It seems to me that many of the benefits of this forgiveness accrue directly to the forgiver because the forgiver receives an attitude of compassion and concern for the forgiven. And since prayer is the discipline of asking, seeking, knocking—of dialogue with God—we are likely to come to discern additional, positive, creative steps we can take toward healing a negative relationship.

HEALING THE RELATIONSHIP BETWEEN NATIONS

The worldwide belief that military might and power bring peace and security for a nation has resulted in one of the great dilemmas facing stewards of creation: never have the people of the earth been so heavily armed as we all are armed today! We are involved in a tremendous arms race, and historians tell us that nearly every other arms race in the past has ended in war.

But the next war will be vastly different from any other the world has experienced! We have harnessed the basic power of the universe and are now capable of hurling that almost unbelievable power against our perceived enemies. As I have pointed out before, nuclear war will bring the instant mass murder of millions, quick death from burns for millions more, and a slower, agonizing death from hunger, thirst, exposure, injuries, and disease to countless others. Survivors, if there are any, will experience cancer, psychological damage, social breakdown, children with birth defects, and poisoning of large parts of the environment. It could well spell the end of the human race and the end of the earth's ecosystem. And so we truthfully say, "The bad news is . . . you might survive!"

Concern over nuclear weapons is not new. Some of the scientists who helped develop the first atomic weapons opposed their use against Japan. After the war, when both the Soviet Union and the United States possessed these awesome weapons, the United Nations Disarmament Commission worked for five years to achieve some kind of arms limitation agreement—to no avail. The movement in the 1980's to freeze the nuclear arms race differs from earlier efforts in a number of ways, but chiefly because this current movement is not limited to a handful of scientists and political leaders but rather is a mass effort by average citizens who have become alarmed at the results of this arms race between nations.

For the first centuries following Jesus' resurrection, the overwhelming majority of Christians followed the way of nonparticipation in violence. No Christian writer during those years tried to justify participation in any kind of war. Tertullian expressed the spirit of those early centuries when he wrote, "Christ in disarming Peter disarmed every soldier."

Only when Christianity was adopted by the Roman Empire in the fourth century did the church compromise Jesus' way of dealing with violence. The church adopted what later became the position of a majority of Christians through the centuries—the justifiable war theory. According to this theory, a justifiable war must meet these standards:

- The war must be the last resort.
- The war must have a just cause—to defend the innocent, to defend against unjust demands, and so forth.
- The war must be declared properly by a properly constituted government.
- There must be a reasonable prospect for victory.
- The means must be proportionate to the ends, not causing unnecessary destruction that outweighs the final good sought.
- Noncombatants are to be safeguarded.
- The defeated are to be shown mercy.

These standards were formulated by Ambrose and Augustine when Christianity became the official religion of the Roman Empire, and they are still the basic stand on war of the majority of Protestant churches, the Eastern Orthodox Church, and the Roman Catholic Church. They are not, however, founded on the Bible or the teachings of Jesus, but on the writings of Plato and Cicero.

Down through the years only a minority of individuals and groups have continued to embrace Jesus' way as completely normative. Unfortunately, Christians who live this way are often accused by other Christians of being weak, cowardly, or unrealistic. The response of one person is compelling:

The Christian whose loyalty to the Prince of Peace puts him or her out of step with today's nationalistic world because of a willingness to love one's nation's friends but not to hate the nation's enemies is not an unrealistic dreamer who thinks that by one's objections all wars will end. It is rather the soldiers who . . . [are unrealistic by thinking] that they can put an end to wars by preparing for just one more. Nor does the Christian think that by refusal to help with the organized destruction of life and property one is uninvolved in the complications and conflicts of modern life. Nor is the Christian reacting simply in emotional fear to the fantastic awefulness of the weapons created by the demonic ingenuity of modern humanity. The Christian loves one's enemies not because he or she thinks they are wonderful people, nor because it is thought that love is sure to conquer them; and not because the believer fails to respect one's native land or its ruler, nor is unconcerned for the safety of one's neighbors, nor because another political or economic system may be favored. The Christian loves his or her enemies because God does, and . . . commands his followers to do so; that is the only reason, and that is enough.

(From "Living the Disarmed Life," by John Howard Yoder, in A Matter of Faith. Sojourners, 1981.)

I do not doubt that most of us Christians accept Jesus' teaching that the way of nonviolent love should be the normal life for us. We know, too, that the task of the church is to follow Christ by working for the goal of peace. At the same time, I know that the justifiable war standards have been used to help us understand that in an evil world there may be rare times when a Christian can, without sin, share in the government's function of protecting its citizens. And most, if not all, of our churches teach that if the government attempts to become involved in an unjustifiable war, the Christian should refuse to participate and endure the punishment that may result as a way of bearing the cross of Christ.

All of this is very difficult to discuss in a large, disorganized group. So I would suggest that you break into small, intergenerational groups and devote most of your time together to Bible study and prayer, asking the Holy Spirit to guide you in peace and gentleness. Determine where people are in relation to the issue of war and peace, violence and nonviolence. Have them share what they clearly understand from Jesus' teachings about love, and where they are struggling.

Consider the seven justifiable war principles as they apply to our current world situation. Do not get lost in World War Two, Korea, or Vietnam. Talk about today and tomorrow. For example, ask the following questions:

1. Are we trying every means possible to negotiate, or are we putting much of our effort into preparations for war?

2. How can we justify a war that most certainly will destroy almost everyone we are supposed to protect?

3. Would time allow a "proper" declaration of war?

4. Is there any chance of winning an all-out nuclear war?

5. Would the resulting destruction of life, property, ecosystems, and perhaps the entire human race be proportionate to the intended goal?

6. Is there any possibility that even tactical battlefield nuclear weapons would avoid mass killing of noncombatants?

7. If anyone could win, would the winner be capable of giving the proper help to the defeated?

Write a group statement entitled "Our Suggestions for a Christian War/Peace Stance in the Nuclear Age." Remember that it is not necessary for your group to reach a consensus. The statement may reflect different views. What is important is that your campers are involved in a process for finding a new ethical stance.

You might encourage members of the group to write to world leaders to tell them of your views. Here are several addresses to get you started:

The President of the U.S.S.R.
c/o The Embassy of the U.S.S.R.
1825 Phelps Place, N.W
Washington, D.C. 20008

The Governor General
Government House
Ottawa, Ontario K1A 0A1

The Prime Minister
Langiven Block
Ottawa, Ontario K1A 0A2

The President of the United States
The White House
Washington, D.C. 20500

(Your member of Parliament)
House of Commons
Ottawa, Ontario K1A 0A9

The Honorable (your senator)
U.S. Senate
Washington, D.C. 20510

The Honorable (your representative)
U.S. House of Representatives
Washington, D.C. 20515

In the United States, congressional offices average 100,000 letters a year. Because of this, your opinions will carry more weight if they are stated concisely. Relatively few Canadian citizens write to their members of Parliament. A recent study estimated that each member of Parliament receives an average of about twenty letters each week. The same study indicated that members assume each letter represents the opinion of approximately one hundred people.

Here are some tips for improving your letters to governmental leaders:

1. Clearly identify the bill or issue. It is important to be specific—refer to its number or popular title.

2. Be timely. Opinions on bills already acted on are too late to do any good.

3. Be brief!

4. State your own views. Form letters, mimeographed petitions, or letters signed by long lists of people are not as effective as personal letters.

5. Give reasons for your position. Tell how it affects your family, your community, people at home or abroad.

6. Be constructive. Suggest a better solution.

WHAT ARE THE ALTERNATIVES TO MILITARY SERVICE?

You will probably spend quite a bit of time with your group discussing the attitude a Christian should hold toward war. As you talk, you will see why this is one of the most difficult and complex ethical questions facing us.

Most of the major denominations have adopted statements on conscientious objection, affirming this position as an appropriate alternative for a Christian. I suggest that you secure a copy of your denomination's statement before camp begins and become familiar with it to guide you in your discussions.

In the past, and presumably in the future, the governments of Canada and the United States have recognized the conscientious objector position, wherein an individual has a deep religious or philosophical basis for his or her opposition to war and killing in any form. It should be pointed out immediately that concientious objectors generally have not sought an easy way out. In fact, many have chosen noncombatant roles in the military service and have distinguished themselves by taking high risks as medical personnel in combat zones.

The governments have not been as open to selective conscientious objection, however, in which a person does not necessarily reject war as such, but may object to serving in a particular war or to engaging in a certain type of warfare. Most denominations appear to believe that selective conscientious objection is ethically and theologically valid.

Any ethical choice we make brings with it certain costs. Those who decide to serve in the military face the possibility of risking their lives in combat. Those who choose conscientious objector status may face criticism and rejection from friends and neighbors and various civil and criminal penalties. Any of these alternatives, if made in good conscience, should receive the spiritual support of the Christian community.

In the process of deciding about one's stand regarding military service, a Christian should be able to draw on the deep resources of the Biblical and theological heritage of the church. Then after long and careful prayer, and deep discussion and thought with trusted friends (perhaps at camp), he or she will arrive at a decision. However, a decision made simply because everyone else has made it, or for one's own convenience, is an insult to one's own conscience in Christ and to the enormity of the issues of war and peace.

To receive literature dealing with disarmament and peacemaking, you can write to any of the following addresses:

NGO Liaison Office
Centre for Disarmament, Room 3577C
United Nations
New York, N.Y. 10017

The Order of St. Martin
16075 Bass Lake Avenue
Gowen, Mich. 49326

Peacemaking Project, Room 1101
Interchurch Center
475 Riverside Drive
New York, N.Y. 10115

Mennonite Central Committee
21 South 12th Street
Akron, Pa. 17501

Ground Zero
806 15th Street, N.W., Suite 421
Washington, D.C. 20025

Canadian Human Rights Foundation
1980 Sherbrooke W., Suite 340
Montreal HSH 1E8

Amnesty International
2101 Algonquin Avenue
Ottawa K2A 1T1

Association for Peace
Box 37, Stn E
Toronto M6H 4E1

Mennonite Central Committee
201–1483 Pembina Highway
Winnipeg, Manitoba R3T 2C8

Committee for Justice and Liberty
229 College Street
Toronto M5T 1R4

HEALING THE RELATIONSHIPS BETWEEN PEOPLE

The sheer volume of Biblical passages that pertain to questions of justice, hunger, and the poor is astonishing! And in these passages God calls us to whom grace has been offered to repent, forsake our self-centered ways, and begin to love our neighbor as ourselves. Our Lord Jesus very clearly pointed out that love for God is inseparable from love for our neighbors. Jesus went on to indicate that anyone in need is our neighbor, not just the folks who happen to live next door!

Therefore our neighbors are people of all races, classes, continents, sexes, and ages. Most of us Christians in Canada and the United States have more than enough of the material things of life, but we should remember the 750 million people in the poorest nations whose income possibility is so low that even as you read this they face death because of malnutrition. And we should not forget the hundreds of millions of other neighbors in developing countries who barely subsist at poverty-level incomes. Nor should we overlook people in our own lands who have not received equal rights for whatever reason.

To help us to be constantly aware of our neighbors and their needs, we need to remember the preacher's call for Christians to take the Bible in one hand and the newspaper in the other. The news media will graphically enlighten us about the many problems facing our neighbors, and the Bible will encourage us to work harder to fulfill their needs as we recall Jesus' words, "Happy are those whose greatest desire is to do what God requires; God will satisfy them fully! Happy are those who are merciful to others; God will be merciful to them!" (*Matt. 5:6-7*).

To get your group of campers started in the healing process, ask someone to read *Ps. 43* aloud. Ask what kind of justice the campers think the psalmist was calling for. Next, have someone read *Isa. 11:1-5*. This is a prophecy of the future hope of Israel. What kind of justice did the writer expect? Finally, ask someone to read *Luke 11:1-4*. What kind of justice did Jesus teach us to ask for in our prayers? What differences and similarities do your campers see in the Old and New Testament writers?

Divide the campers up into small discussion groups. A good way to do this is by having everyone whose birthday is in January form a group, February another group, and so forth. Assign each group a social problem to discuss for thirty minutes (one member of each group should keep notes), then call them all back together for a report session.

Examples of social problems might include the following:

Drug abuse in the community
Unemployment
Vandalism, muggings, rapes
Hunger in the local community
Racial strife and discrimination
Local church refusing to call a woman minister
Hunger in a neighboring country
Restrictive immigration laws and quotas
Lack of decent housing in the local community
Poor schools in some parts of the community
Lack of care for the elderly and handicapped
Low wages for women and youth

What kinds of local projects can you and your campers get involved in back home? Check with your pastor, look for announcements of special programs in the newspapers, and watch public service announcements on television. How can you support and encourage one another? How will you handle problems that are bound to arise? How can you enlist others to your cause? How can you be sure of God's will in this situation?

JUSTICE FOR WILDLIFE

We have earlier considered God's call to each one of us to be a steward of creation. In both the Creation poem in *Gen. 1:1 to 2:4* (a religious affirmation of God as creator, and probably written in this form by priests between 600 and 500 B.C.), and the Creation story in *Gen. 2:5 to 3:24* (put into written form around 1200 B.C.) we human beings are given responsibility for caring for all other life on earth. Neither the poem nor the story pretends to be a scientific account of Creation. You can avoid confusion for your campers if you will help them understand that these Biblical accounts are less concerned with how the world was created than with who masterminded the creative process and how good and evil came into the world.

Saint Francis was very much aware of his sisters and brothers in the animal kingdom. Many of the rest of us have forgotten them or have looked at them only as a source of food, clothing, or entertainment.

For example, in 1900, about 5 million elephants roamed the African continent, compared with only an estimated 1.3 million today. Huge numbers of elephants have been killed for their ivory tusks. Considered a hedge against inflation, ivory increased in value from $3.00 a pound in 1960 to $150.00 a pound in 1980. During the 1970's, hunters in search of ivory profits killed about half the elephants in eastern Africa. The development of land for farms and factories also destroys the elephants' habitat and further threatens these animals that need 400 pounds of food daily.

Whales are another large animal in danger. Some whales may eat over a ton of krill (tiny marine crustaceans) in one feeding and are still much sought after for their meat and blubber and for other parts of their bodies, which are used for a wide variety of products, from pet food to expensive perfume. Thirty-nine nations have joined the International Whaling Commission, and in 1982 voted to end commercial whaling as of 1986. Conservationists have been cautiously jubilant because this apparent victory could be reversed at any time for at least three years. Very small quotas for bowhead (17), gray (179), and humpback (10) whales will still be allowed each year for food for Alaskan, Siberian, and Greenland Eskimos, whose very lives depend on this food source.

Grizzly bears have not fared as well as the whales so far. Unless both Canada and the United States do something soon to stop illegal hunting and to control land developments in their habitats, much of the grizzly bear population of North America is in danger of being lost. In the United States, for example, the grizzly population has fallen from 50,000 west of the Mississippi (but excluding Alaska) at the beginning of the eighteenth century to fewer than 1,000 today.

Another danger facing wildlife, especially birds, was caused by an unwitting human error of more than thirty years ago. According to wildlife biologists, the powerful insecticide DDT very nearly wiped out the total population of some of our bird friends.

In the years following World War Two, the chemical was widely used to attack insect pests from mosquitoes to fleas. Dusted onto crops or into marshes, it found its way into topsoil and groundwater, ultimately entering the life systems of all living creatures. But certain birds of prey such as peregrine falcons, bald eagles, hawks, owls, vultures, and pelicans were especially affected. Being at the top of the food chain, these birds accumulated heavy doses of DDT.

Biologists say that DDT poisoning sickens mature birds. But a greater danger was that the chemical attacked the reproductive system of the birds, producing a phenomenon known as eggshell thinning. The birds laid eggs with shells so thin that the weight of a brooding parent would crush them.

When laboratory tests identified DDT as the cause of the plunge in the large-bird population, the chemical was banned from use in much of North America. For such birds as bald eagles and pelicans, the ban came just in time. But ornithologists fear that the populations of some other birds have been decimated past the point of return unless human intervention can restore what human mistakes have damaged.

Aerial spraying of DDT in Canada also caused the death of hundreds of thousands of trout and salmon. A count made over several years in the Miramichi Basin, New Brunswick, showed that DDT, sprayed in adjacent forests, poisoned or starved two thirds of the salmon. There were no young fish in 1954 or 1956, while insects preying on the forests thrived after each treatment. In British Columbia almost 100 percent of the salmon perished in some areas.

Fortunately, groups have been formed to aid in the struggle to save and increase our remaining wildlife populations, Novel techniques are used, such as artificial insemination to increase birth rates and closed-circuit television to monitor wildlife living areas to help keep down human contact so the birds and other animals will retain most of their natural instincts. You can secure literature from these groups, and some of them will provide speakers or films for use in your camp programs.

With your campers you can start to identify and list the species of animals that live on or near your campsite. A number of excellent field guide books are available. Note the habitats, life cycles, and interrelationships of the animals you find. Go on hikes, sit on a stump, or wait in a blind as you make daily observations. You can try making plaster casts of animal tracks you locate. Look for nests and dens. Observe the feeding habits and food of the animals and birds you see. Keep a record of all the information you gather. Combine it with pictures (somebody in the group can probably draw fairly well) in a book and leave it at camp for "future generations."

Discuss with your campers what each of you will do to aid your fellow living creatures in their uphill struggle against extermination. For ideas, in advance of the camp session, write for literature to the following organizations:

Center for Environmental Education
624 9th Street, N.W.
Washington, D.C. 20001

Canadian Wildlife Federation
1673 Carling Avenue
Ottawa, Ontario K2A 1C4

World Wildlife Fund
910 17th Street, N.W.
Washington, D.C. 20006

Department of the Environment
Oxbridge Place
9820 106 Street
Edmonton, T5K 2J6

The Friends of Animals
11 West 60th Street
New York, N.Y. 10023

Nature Conservancy of Canada
2180 Yonge Street, Ste. 1704
Toronto M4S 2E7

For your Bible study, you can use passages like *Job 39:13-18; Job 39:27-30; Jer. 8:7; Prov. 30:24-28.*

TOWARD A COMMITMENT TO STEWARDSHIP

In recent years the popular press has devoted a great deal of its energy (to say nothing of paper and ink) to publishing guides to help us in our search for self-fulfillment. For some of us it has taken years to realize that there are at least two major flaws in the current self-fulfillment strategy: (1) the concept that the "self" is totally a collection of inner needs, and (2) the idea that economic security and some kind of recognized power are necessary to satisfy those needs. Those of us who study the history of humanity can see that thousands of years of experience clearly indicate that the truth is quite the opposite.

As we have already seen, between now and A.D. 2000 we North Americans are going to be called on to make many changes in our life-styles. Some of these changes may be painful as we try to accommodate to new economic and political realities. If we interpret these changes as an indication of failure, we may accept them as unpleasant but necessary, or we may become angry, resentful, and resistant. On the other hand, if we see these changes as a new commitment to the stewardship role to which we have always been called by Almighty God, then they will signify a gain in the quality of our life-style, not just an adjustment to loss.

So we now need to make a new commitment to our stewardship! You will probably observe that a number of your campers are already involved in a search for such a commitment as they attempt to shift the center of their lives away from self-fulfillment toward a connectedness with the world. Many will express a hunger for deeper personal relationships as they recognize that, although they may have many acquaintances, they have few close friends. Most of them also share with us a deep yearning to reach out for involvements that go deeper than the surface, a willingness to sacrifice some of the material values for the sake of real, meaningful involvement as stewards of creation.

Guidelines for a simpler life-style as stewards of creation cannot be laid down in universal rules; they must be developed by individuals and communities according to their own situation and interpretation of Scripture. A simpler life-style is not a panacea, but it can be significant in our commitment to the stewardship of creation if embarked upon for some or all of the following reasons listed by the Division for Peace, Justice, and Human Rights of the Lutheran World Federation:

1. As an *act of faith* performed for the sake of personal integrity and as an expression of personal commitment to a more equitable distribution of the world's resources.

2. As an *act of self-defense* against the mind-and-body-polluting effects of overconsumption.

3. As an *act of withdrawal* from the achievement neurosis of our high-pressure, materialistic societies.

4. As an *act of solidarity* with the majority of humankind, which has no choice about life-style.

5. As an *act of sharing* with others what has been given to us, or of returning what was usurped by us through unjust social and economic structures.

6. As an *act of celebration* of the riches found in creativity, spirituality, and community with others, rather than in mindless materialism.

7. As an *act of provocation* (ostentatious underconsumption) to arouse curiosity leading to dialogue with others about affluence, alienation, poverty, and social injustices.

8. As an *act of anticipation* of the era when the self-confidence and assertiveness of the underprivileged forces new power relationships and new patterns of resource allocation upon us.

9. As an *act of advocacy* of legislated changes in present patterns of production and consumption in the direction of a new international economic order.

10. As an *exercise of purchasing power* to redirect production away from the satisfaction of artificially created wants toward the supplying of goods and services that meet genuine social needs.

The best formal statement I know of for making a written commitment to be a steward of creation is the Shakertown Pledge, which follows:

The Shakertown Pledge

Recognizing that the earth and the fullness thereof is a gift from our gracious God, and that we are called to cherish, nurture, and provide loving stewardship for the earth's resources,

And recognizing that life itself is a gift, and a call to responsibility, joy, and celebration, I make the following declarations:

1. I declare myself to be a world citizen.

2. I commit myself to lead an ecologically sound life.

3. I commit myself to lead a life of creative simplicity and to share my personal wealth with the world's poor.

4. I commit myself to join with others in reshaping institutions in order to bring about a more just global society in which each person has full access to the needed resources for his/her physical, emotional, intellectual, and spiritual growth.

5. I commit myself to occupational accountability, and in so doing I will seek to avoid the creation of products which cause harm to others.

6. I affirm the gift of my body, and commit myself to its proper nourishment. and physical well-being.

7. I commit myself to examine continually my relations with others, and to attempt to relate honestly, morally, and lovingly to those around me.

8. I commit myself to personal renewal through prayer, meditation, and study.

9. I commit myself to responsible participation in a community of faith.

(From *A Covenant Group for Lifestyle Assessment,* by William E. Gibson. United Presbyterian Program Agency, 1981.)

AN ETHIC TO LIVE BY

In the concluding pages of Sigurd Olson's *Of Time and Place,* written shortly before his death in 1982, the author wrote:

All the places I have written about are part of the total picture of the earth and how we feel toward it. We ask ourselves if we are doing what is right. Are we good stewards? Have we done all we can to stop ugliness, devastation, and decay in the world around us? . . . Ethical and moral questions and how we answer them may determine whether primeval scenes will continue to be a source of joy and comfort to future generations. The decisions are ours and we have to search our minds and souls for the right answers. We must ask ourselves how we truly feel about what we have done to the planet during our brief tenure upon it. Are we really willing to do what we should, and are we mature enough to forget selfish interests? When critical areas are being threatened, will we stand up and fight for them no matter how unpopular such stands might be? Our most important goal is preservation of the land which is our home. We must be eternally vigilant and embrace the broad concept of an environmental ethic to survive.

(From *Of Time and Place,* by Sigurd F. Olson. Alfred A. Knopf, 1982.)

PART FOUR:
Additional Resources

12.
Appendix

MODEL—THE FINDHORN GARDEN

Since its founding in 1962, the Findhorn Garden, located in Scotland on a sandy peninsula jutting out into the North Sea, has been visited by doubting horticulturists and curious tourists. These visitors have come away telling of their amazement to find a patch of sand and gravel developed into a flourishing garden with over 128 varieties of vegetables, herbs, and fruit. They also have told of the tiny group which has turned a run-down mobile home park into a model community. But most intriguing is the idea that these social, physical, and botanical achievements have been accomplished through meditation and communication with the spirit and forces of nature. The spirit of the Findhorn Community insists that it is love that makes plants as well as people grow.

Many of us have problems with the insistence of the residents of the Findhorn Community that the original gardeners were advised by God's voice through Eileen, the devas speaking through Dorothy, the nature spirits through Roc, and other levels of reality contacted by David. But we can understand that the hours of hard labor, the creation and addition of rich compost, and the care expressed for all living things have really paid off.

Although I do not accept most of the spiritual concepts espoused by the Findhorn Community, I do agree that love for all other living things is primary to becoming a true steward of creation, and I recommend reading *The Findhorn Garden* to gain information for discussion. (*The Findhorn Garden,* by The Findhorn Community, Harper & Row, 1975, published simultaneously by Fitzhenry and Whiteside, Limited, Toronto.)

MODEL—THE COMMUNITY OF CHRIST

Established in 1965 in Washington, D.C., the Community of Christ is an ecumenical Christian fellowship whose members have covenanted to join in common discipline, common ministries, and common witness. The fellowship selected the term *community* for its name as a way of emphasizing people instead of a building, because they do not own any property or live together, although most live within an area of about one square mile around Dupont Circle, a mile from the White House.

Once this was an area of substantial, white middle-class townhouses, but now most of these buildings have been converted into rooming houses and small apartment complexes filled with young workers and students, black families, and the aged who are clinging to the old neighborhood. The fellowship has grown to about sixty adults and thirty-five children. As a group they conduct six worship services a week, usually in the homes of members, and each member of the fellowship attempts to attend at least one of these services each week.

The common discipline involves daily prayer and meditation periods, which include intercession for others of the Community by name, weekly participation in worship and Communion, weekly periods of study together, a financial pledge of proportionate giving to the needs of the world, and a promise to be open to God's call and to participate in at least one spiritual life retreat each year. These disciplines are voluntary and are reviewed every six months.

The common ministry involves trying to be a good neighbor and responding to those around the community with personal interaction and human warmth. The community has learned that the needs of individuals are frequently related to the institutions in which they live their daily lives, so the community has become involved in attempting to alter these institutions, including the government.

The Community of Christ has decided not to attempt to make the present system more responsive or efficient, but rather to attempt the radical alteration of the system in a peaceful manner. They tell us that the form to accomplish mission is "up for grabs" at any given time and that a cognitive minority can make great demands on both society and ecclesiastical institutions and have them met. Therefore, the community pledges most of its budget to be used for others, often for food, clothing, and housing. Community members seek their own housing and employment.

A full description of the Community of Christ can be read in *Dance in Steps of Change,* by John Schramm and David Anderson (Thomas Nelson, Inc., 1970).

MODEL—L'ABRI

Located in the tiny Swiss Alpine village of Huémoz, L'Abri (the term is French for "shelter") is a spiritual shelter, based on Christian traditions, for any in need of spiritual help. Its cofounders, Dr. Francis A. Schaeffer and his wife, Edith, are particularly concerned about providing a sheltering community for those who are seeking answers to the basic philosophical problems with which all of us who care about finding a purpose in life have to struggle.

Participants come from an international background, a wide age range, and a wide variety of religious beliefs. Workers at L'Abri believe that each person who comes is an answer to a definite prayer that God will choose who is to come and keep all others away.

Those who come to study spend four hours each morning listening to tape-recorded lectures, discussions, sermons, or Bible studies. Another four hours each day are spent in practical housekeeping work around the L'Abri buildings. There are two live lectures a week as well as a Sunday service of worship and high tea and Bible study on Sunday evening. There are also occasional musical evenings and opportunities for personal conversations in front of the fireplace or around the dinner table.

Financially, L'Abri lives on a "shoestring" budget but makes no appeals for funds (in fact, does no advertising whatsoever). Students who come in answer to prayer contribute a small daily fee. Workers receive no salary other than room and board and a small monthly gift if there is any money left over after paying rents, utilities, and food costs.

It is generally expected that L'Abri students will not remain at the center in Switzerland for a prolonged period but will remain as a part of the extended community when they return to their homes. As an outgrowth of this, small L'Abri centers have developed in a number of other countries, and the work and teachings of the Schaeffers are now widely known. Quite simply, the teaching of L'Abri is that God has, time after time, answered prayer in the midst of well-nigh impossible circumstances to bring something out of nothing.

A very personal account of the history and ministry of L'Abri is contained in Edith Schaeffer's book, *L'Abri* (published by Tyndale House, 1969, and distributed in Canada by Home Evangel Books Ltd., Toronto, Ontario).

MODEL—THE SHAKERS

For more than two hundred years the American Shakers have lived in simplicity and unity in Christian communal families. They liberated women, welcomed all races, opposed war, perfected their quiet arts and crafts, worshiped God as Mother and Father, and expressed religious joy and love of each other by dancing and singing.

In 1774 Mother Ann (1736–1784) led a group of fellow believers from England to North America and founded the first communistic organization in the United States. They were an offshoot of a sect that had broken away from the Quakers. Members of the new United Society of Believers are called Shakers because as a part of their worship they quiver, tremble, and shake while chanting wordless songs. Shakers do not marry or bear children. The sect is kept alive only through converts.

Noted in the past for their fine farms and ingenuity, the Shakers invented the circular saw, cut nails, flat brooms, metal pen points, and a type of washing machine. The fine furniture they produced is now prized by collectors.

The Shakers have made many important contributions to our way of life, but they now have fewer than twenty-five members living in Canterbury, New Hampshire, and Sabbathday Lake, Maine. The village referred to as "Shakertown" is now called Pleasant Hill, Kentucky.

A SAMPLE DEVOTIONAL SERVICE

Song

Leader: Gracious God, who are in the world and surpass the world, blessed be your presence in us.

Group: You have shown yourself to be the God of life by entering into a covenant agreement with all your living creatures. You lead the whole of creation to salvation in these signs that the covenant agreement is reestablished—

Leader: From nothing to creation,
Across floods to mountaintop,
Through sea to dry land,
Up from slavery to freedom,
From desert to green pastures,
After fast to feast, and
Through war to peace.

Group: You care for the world, guiding it—

Leader: From sickness to health,
Beyond night to day,
From seed to fruitful tree,
From rain to shine,
From winter to springtime,
By the cross to new life, and
Out of the grave to victory.

Song

Scripture Lessons. Some suggested passages are the following:

Gen. 1:26-31a	James 2:14-18	Matt. 25:14-30
Isa. 3:13-15	Lev. 19:9-10	Luke 6:20-26
Ezek. 34:17-27	Isa. 58:3-7	I John 3:11-18
Luke 3:9-11		

Meditation

Prayer

Leader: Let us consider how we have used the resources of the world that God has given us. Let us help one another see whether we have created the systems necessary to protect and preserve these resources and the precious life God has given to us. Let us pray for the church and for the family of humankind, and especially for all who suffer.

Group: Lord, hear our prayer.

Leader: For all in this community, that we may have the courage to examine our habits of consumption, and to restrain ourselves so we are in solidarity with our brothers and sisters who are in need, let us pray to the Lord.

Group: Lord, hear our prayer.

Leader: For those who are experimenting with new methods of crop production, that our support and resources may better serve our brothers and sisters through them, let us pray to the Lord.

Group: Lord, hear our prayer.

Leader: For all who personally feed the hungry and clothe the poor on our behalf, in thanksgiving for their witness, let us pray to the Lord.

Group: Lord, hear our prayer.

Leader: For those who are developing new ways to preserve the land, to clean up the air and the water, that the lives of all God's children can be free of unseen poisons, let us pray to the Lord.

Group: Lord, hear our prayer.

Leader: For all who speak to any government in behalf of peace and justice, that the leaders of the world will know and do God's will with strength and courage, let us pray to the Lord.

Group: Lord, hear our prayer.

Leader: For our loved ones, and for all people everywhere, that they may be sensitive and responsive to the needs of all other people, let us pray to the Lord.

Group: Lord, hear our prayer. Amen.

Leader: Our God hears our prayers and forgives our sins. Through Christ we are reconciled with God; therefore, through Christ let us be reconciled with one another and share the peace of the Lord.

Sharing of the Peace

Song

SUGGESTIONS FOR INDIVIDUAL ACTION

One of the big questions that will come up at camp in any discussion of the stewardship of creation is "What can I do when I get home?"

As program facilitators we can help our campers of whatever age understand that ordinary people *can* do something. Each person has special abilities. Not to use them is to bury your talents as did the servant in Jesus' parable; to use them is to offer yourself to God and to reach out to others. Although individual efforts may be difficult to measure, they do make a difference. They are like the small ripples that in combination with others add up to big waves.

It is easy for an individual to get discouraged, particularly when the newness wears off and the enthusiasm generated at camp fades. It is better to start small and stick with it than to start big and drop out of the race. It will help if camp leaders can assist each individual camper to select one thing to start with at once, not waiting for a better time to come along.

Here is a list of things an individual can do. Like most lists, it does not include everything, and you may want to make additions and improvements. The suggestions are not all easy, but they are within reach.

1. Become a citizen advocate. Communicate with your member of Congress/Parliament and with other appropriate leaders about key issues.

2. Support your denomination's hunger and peace appeals. Our church agencies are very effective and deserve greatly increased support in prayers and dollars.

3. Become better informed. Read books, magazine articles, and newspapers. The better informed you are, the more effective you will be.

4. Interest others. Share what you have learned and how you feel.

5. Discuss world problems with your family or household. Parents, especially, do themselves and their children a great favor by putting these issues front-and-center in family discussions.

6. Write an occasional letter to the editor. Be brief and to the point. Choose a specific issue—preferably one that has been reported or commented on editorially.

7. Reassess your own life's pattern. Perhaps you can consume, waste, eat, drink, drive, heat, or air-condition less. Fast occasionally (many denominations have scheduled occasional fast days) and use the money saved for hunger relief.

8. Help form a local discussion group. If one already exists, take part. Push especially for effective responses on public issues.

9. Work for legislation that will help overcome world problems.

10. Pray. Pray daily for those who do not have enough; for those who lead; for the wisdom to see your own part in the problem and its solution; and for the grace to take appropriate action.

SPECIAL CONCERNS FOR SENIOR ADULTS

For a great many senior adults, living a simpler life-style is not a matter of choice—it is a real necessity brought on by the stresses of the economy today. When inflation keeps raising the cost of living, having to get by on a fixed income can be a frightening experience. The loss of control over one's life is one of the greatest fears that many elderly people face. They see themselves as gradually being forced to turn over the right to make decisions that affect their lives to others, growing more and more dependent and less in control of their own lives.

Most of the activities in this resource book are suitable for senior adults, and others can easily be adapted for their use. In the first place, senior adults do not need to be convinced that being a good steward or being in charge of one's own life is a goal to strive toward. Most of them can appreciate better than some younger folks the value of belonging to a caring community of faith. They also have a great deal of wisdom to share and will appreciate channels for doing that. The time they spend at camp in a program on stewardship of creation will open new vistas for giving and receiving, and this can be life-changing!

In planning a program that includes senior adults, you should bear in mind several factors that are often related to this age group:

1. You will need to overcome the image of "roughing it," which is usually associated with camps, such as sagging bunk beds, poor toilet facilities at a distance from sleeping areas, dim light, and cold rooms. In fact, today many camps and retreat centers provide very comfortable accommodations. Be sure you arrange for them!

2. For various reasons you will find that not all camp buildings or areas are accessible to persons with some physical handicaps. Be sure to visit the camp in advance of signing a contract!

3. Senior adults often need more rest than their younger counterparts, so be sure to include frequent breaks for free time in the schedule.

4. Some senior adults (as well as other campers) may require special diets. Check to see that the food service staff can handle this. What arrangements need to be made in advance?

5. Be sure you know the whereabouts of nearby medical facilities and how to call for emergency paramedics and evacuation. It is a good idea to make personal contact with a local doctor in advance of need to arrange for his or her services.

6. Schedule some quieter games and activities that are not too physically demanding. Allow more time for walks than you would with younger groups.

7. Be sure that you have an adequate amplification system if you are using a large room. Always speak slowly, clearly, and distinctly.

There are also some great program benefits you should remember to incorporate if you are planning for senior adults:

1. Their values are well established and clear. They know what is really important in life and what is not.

2. They have developed many "survival skills," which they are willing to share with others. Many lessons learned in the Great Depression, various dust bowls, and during wartime are still applicable today.

3. Storytelling is an art many senior citizens developed before the advent of television. You can use this skill by encouraging them to share their memories of their rich experiences. I have included some starter ideas at the end of this section.

4. A great many senior adults are very talented when it comes to handcrafts—knitting, crocheting, needlepoint, tatting, whittling, carving, model building, and so forth. Some of them will be expert gardeners, carpenters, plumbers, and so on. Let them pass these skills on to following generations during the relaxed afternoon and evening hours. Be sure to announce these opportunities well in advance so the proper tools and materials will be available at camp.

As you plan your camp schedule, you might also consider adding some special-interest workshops (which can be led by community resource people available in your area), such as the following:

1. Safety and security precautions—how to make your home a safer and more comfortable place to live; ways to alert neighbors to your special needs.

2. Overcoming stress, one of the leading causes of death today.

3. Proper nutrition—how to eat better for less, and why to take time to eat correctly now that you are alone.

4. Money management—ways to get "safe" help in managing what you have.

5. Wills and trusts—how to make decisions about the final distribution of your property, and what the advantages are of a "living trust" agreement with a church-related agency.

6. Community agencies that can help the elderly, and the benefits available to everyone.

7. Opportunities for senior adults to be of service to others, for example, foster grandparents, tutoring programs after school, pen pals, Gray Panthers, short-term mission helpers overseas, and so forth. Do not forget the work needed at the local church or in the camp. We have had several senior adults spend a number of months with us working in the office or on building maintenance.

8. Retirement homes available through church agencies—what will happen to me when I am no longer able to care for myself?

MEMORY EVENTS

History books are filled with the events of the past, some interesting, some boring. No one can rediscover exactly how things were, but the more we explain about our past, the more we learn about our present and our future.

This is an activity you can do several times during the camp session, using different topics and questions. Gather a "panel of experts" (preferably some of your older campers) and ask them to answer out loud some of these questions:

1. Grandma's house (or the home of another relative)

Did you go to Grandma's on a certain day, or at a certain time of year? What day or time? Why?

How did you get there? What was unusual about it?

What special foods did Grandma cook? Tell about them.

In what ways were you entertained? Were they different from your usual forms of amusement? How?

2. Holidays

How did your family spend holidays when you were a child?

What holidays did your family celebrate? Why?

What presents or other surprises were part of your holiday celebrations?

Did religion play a part in your celebration? In what ways?

3. The good things about your childhood

What did you and your friends do for fun?

What special games did you play? Can you teach us one this week?

What was your favorite toy? Why? How did you receive it? Who made it?

What did you like most about your hometown? Why?

4. Meals in your childhood

Where in your home did you eat most of your meals? How about special meals? With whom did you eat?

What kinds of food did you have at the various meals?

What was your favorite food? Why? What is your favorite today? Why?

Who served, cooked, cleared the table, and did the dishes? How was this decided?

THE TIME MACHINE

Time travel has always been an absorbing subject for many of us. Use this activity with small groups and ask them to use their imaginations to go forward two hundred years in time. Have each person decide what he or she would bring along from each of the following categories to share with the future generation. However, the baggage compartment on your time machine is very small and can hold only one item from each category, so the total group will have to decide on one representative item from each category. Make a list.

When you arrive at the date two hundred years from now, you will find that the future generation still has the same categories but their specific representative items will be different from ours today. Dream about this a bit and then make up a list of items the future generation will want to share with you.

Baggage for the Time Machine		
Category	Present Item	Future's Item
Book Food Religious text Clothing Work of art Child's toy Musical instrument Government document Sample of music Method of communication		

13.
Bibliography

General Reading on Stewardship of Creation

Barney, Gerald O., *The Global Two Thousand Report to the President: Entering the Twenty-first Century.* 3 Vols. Pergamon Press, 1980.

Barney, Gerald O., et al., *Global Two Thousand: Implications for Canada.* Pergamon Press, 1981.

Bisset, Mary Jane, and Oostenbrink, Anja, *Creation and Re-creation: A Congregational Kit.* United Church Press, 1984.

Hall, Douglas John, *The Steward: A Biblical Symbol Come of Age.* Friendship Press, 1982.

Olson, Sigurd, *Of Time and Place.* Alfred A. Knopf, 1982.

Van Matre, Steve, *Acclimatization: A Sensory and Conceptual Approach to Ecological Involvement.* American Camping Association, 1972.

Wilkinson, Loren, *Earthkeeping: Christian Stewardship of Natural Resources.* 2d Ed. William B. Eerdmans, 1980.

Books on Intergenerational Programs

Beissert, Marguerite, *Intergenerational Manual for Christian Education: Shared Approaches.* United Church Press, 1977.

Griggs, Donald and Patricia, *Generations Learning Together.* Abingdon, 1976.

Kehnle, Paul and Barbara, *Intergenerational Camping.* Division for Parish Services of The Lutheran Church in America, 1982.

Kochler, George E., *Learning Together.* Discipleship Resources, 1977.

Kortrey, Barbara (ed.), *Together.* Fortress Press, 1981.

Books on Food Issues

Bailey, Covert, *Fit or Fat?* Houghton Mifflin Co., 1978.

Brown, Lester R., with Eckholm, Eric P., *By Bread Alone.* Praeger, 1976.

Cramer, Craig, *Planning Food Experiences.* Discipleship Resources, 1980.

Food, Fuel and Future. Fortress Press, 1978.

Lappe, Frances Moore, *Diet for a Small Planet.* Ballantine, 1975.

Lappe, Frances Moore, and Collins, Joseph, *World Hunger: Ten Myths.* Institute for Food and Development Policy, 1979.

Minear, Larry, *New Hope for the Hungry?* Friendship Press, 1975.

Simon, Arthur, *Bread for the World.* Paulist Press, 1975.

Books on Land Issues

Fritsch, Albert J., *Environmental Ethics.* Anchor Books, 1980.

Malone, Tom, *Rejoicing with Creation.* John Knox Press, 1979.

Pactkau, Paul, with Harder, Gary, and Sawatzky, Don, *God/Man/Land.* Faith and Life Press, 1978.

Stone, Glenn C., *A New Ethic for a New Earth*. Friendship Press, 1971.
Udall, Steward L., *The Quiet Crisis*. Avon, 1963.
Wilkinson, Loren (ed.), *Earth Keeping*. William B. Eerdmans Publishing Co., 1980.
Witt, Ted R., *Responsible with Creation*. John Knox Press, 1979.

Books on Energy Issues

Better Homes and Gardens Editors, *Energy-saving Projects You Can Build*. Meredith Publishing Co., 1979.
Campbell, Stu, and Taff, Doug, *Build Your Own Solar Water Heater*. Garden Way Publishing, 1978.
Energy Alternatives. Time-Life Books, 1982.
Fritsch, Albert J. (ed.), *Ninety-nine Ways to a Simple Lifestyle*. Center for Science in the Public Interest, Anchor Press, 1977.
Handbook of Homemade Power. Mother Earth News, Bantam Books, 1974.
Parks, Jack, *Simplified Wind Power Systems for Experimenters*. Helion, 1975.
Pierson, Richard E., *Technician's and Experimenter's Guide to Using Sun, Wind, and Water Power*. Parker Publishing, 1978.
Ridgeway, James, *Energy-efficient Community Planning: A Guide to Saving Energy and Producing Power at the Local Level*. JG Press, 1979.
Spiess, Henry R., et al., *350 Ways to Save Energy (and Money) in Your Home and Car*. Crown Publishers, 1974.

Books on Peace and Justice Issues

Ground Zero, *Nuclear War—What's in It for You?* Pocket Books, 1982.
Longacre, Doris Janzen, *Living More with Less*. Herald Press, 1980.
Nelson, Jack A., *Hunger for Justice*. Orbis Books, 1981.
Sider, Ronald J., *Cry Justice*. Paulist Press, 1980.

For Films and Filmstrips on Creation Issues, Contact:

Bread for the World, 32 Union Square East, New York, NY 10003
Bullfrog Films, Inc., Oley, PA 19547
Communication Commission, 475 Riverside Drive, New York, NY 10115
DEC, 121 Avenue Road, Toronto, Ontario M5R 2G3
Enterpriser, 47 Denshy Ave., Toronto, Ontario
Franciscan Communications, 1229 S. Santee, Los Angeles, CA 90015
IDEA Centre, 418 Wardlaw Ave., Winnepeg, Manitoba
Institute for the Study of Peace, 3801 W. Pine St., St. Louis, MO 63108
LCA Audio Visuals, 600 Jarvis St., Toronto, Ontario M4Y 2J6
Maryknoll Library, 25358 Cypress Ave., Hayward, CA 94544
Mass Media Ministries, 2116 North Charles St., Baltimore, MD 21218
National CROP Office, Box 968, Elkhart, IN 46514
Time-Life Films, 100 Eisenhower Dr., Paramus, NJ 07652
UN Films, Box 7316, Alexandria, VA 22307